The 5-M Meditator

Eric Harrison

THE 5-MINUTE MEDITATOR

Copyright © 2005 by Eric Harrison

The first edition of this book was published in 2003 by Judy Piatkus (Publishers) Ltd, London. This is the fully revised, full colour, second edition, published in Australia by Perth Meditation Centre.

ISBN 0-9757716-0-4

Second edition

Size: 223 x 158 mm

No of pages: 176

Publisher: Perth Meditation Centre

Design by John Cooper and Rozz Synnot from:

A Very Useful Design Service
West Perth Ph: 08 9321 0474

www.designservice.com.au

Printed by Picton Press, West Perth

Distributed by Brumby Books, Victoria

www.brumbybooks.com

Ph: 03 9761 5535

Perth Meditation Centre
P O Box 1019, Subiaco, WA 6904
Phone 08 9381 4877
www.perthmeditationcentre.com.au
For information on courses, books and CDs,
see the back pages of this book.

Contents

PART THREE: DO WHAT YOU ARE DOING

PART FOUR: EXERCISE

PART FIVE: PUTTING IT TOGETHER

Introduction

Meditation – the art of relaxing the body quickly and calming the mind – is based on simple principles and is remarkably easy to do. By learning to meditate, we reclaim a skill often lost since childhood: the ability to relax at will and return to a state of balance at any time in the day.

People meditate for many reasons:

> to relax, de-stress and fall asleep;
>
> to improve their health;
>
> for stillness and peace;
>
> to be centred and aware all day long;
>
> for mental clarity and focus;
>
> for inspiration and vision;
>
> to cope with pain and sadness;
>
> to find beauty and meaning in life.

Meditation can show us who we are and how to act intelligently in a less than intelligent world. It has been at the centre of my life for thirty-five years now and I can't imagine anything more valuable.

So why don't we all do more of it? Most people will say they haven't got the time. Since 1987, I've taught meditation to some 25,000 people from all walks of life, mostly in courses of seven weeks duration. I've taught business executives, housewives, tradesmen and children. I've trained doctors, psychologists and teachers to share this skill with others. I've taught athletes and performers, and also the ill and dying.

Typically they say they can't find the time to meditate, even the retired and the seriously ill. If you think of meditation as thirty minutes of sitting still and 'doing nothing', you may well feel you're too busy or too stressed to do it. The common refrain is 'I know I should do more of it but...'

In fact, meditation is easy to integrate into almost any day, once you know how. Over the years, I've taught what I call 'spot-meditations' that are very short and can be done anywhere and anytime. You can easily relax while walking, eating or doing exercise or housework. You can use the 'waste' time, when you're waiting, or in public transport or trying to fall asleep at night. I personally do twenty to fifty spot-meditations a day.

I developed these meditations as much for my own sake as for my students'. Twenty years ago, I spent eighteen months in retreat in the Southern Alps of New Zealand, and in the wilds of New South Wales. This experience proved to be the great turning point in my life, yet at the time I was afraid that my clarity of mind would disintegrate once I returned to earning a living and relating to the opposite sex. I seriously wondered if tranquility was only possible in seclusion and was quite unattainable in the city.

I found that spot-meditations gave me the answer. By relaxing rapidly for a minute or two, many times a day, I can stop the daily challenges overwhelming me. I think more clearly and am more attuned to what I am doing. Since spot-meditations also enhance sensory awareness, I am often 'ambushed by beauty' and 'surprised by joy', even during the most pedestrian of days. By keeping the substrata of my mind clean, they even make my long meditations more satisfying.

People who meditate regularly know the good results percolate somewhat through the hours that follow. However the effect of the previous night's long meditation is vanishingly faint compared to what a spot-meditation can do for you right now.

By meditating 'on the spot', I find I don't need stress-free surroundings and an introverted life for a good quality of mind. These modest little exercises have far exceeded my expectations and have taken me in directions I never imagined possible. The Buddha got it wrong when he said that a secluded, celibate life is essential. I'm now a far more sophisticated meditator and a wiser person than when I lived in the wilderness.

JUST BE HERE

Spot-meditations have an ancient history. The Buddha himself said 'Be calm and aware while walking, eating, dressing, urinating or lying down to sleep.' He exhorted us to make use of each day and whatever situation we find ourselves in, good or bad. He also gave remarkably lucid instructions about how to do this although few people, even serious Buddhist meditators, know what they are or follow them systematically.

On the other hand, the idea of 'being present', or 'doing what you are doing' is quite familiar to many. Those trained in Buddhism or Yoga know it under the name of 'awareness' or 'mindfulness'. In hippie times it was encapsulated in the slogan 'Be Here Now'. It is a commonplace idea, even in Western thought, that to be happy you should 'live for the day'. Gurus of various persuasions often take the idea to absurd lengths by saying that the past and future are illusions, and enlightenment is all about 'the now'.

I've found however, that the idea of 'being present' usually remains just an idea. People use it as a slogan, but it hardly ever affects their behaviour. Even people who do ten-day 'Awareness' retreats or practise Zen still tend to think of meditation as the long, silent sittings in seclusion and rarely apply the principle to their ordinary lives.

Two-minute meditations, even if you do dozens of them, have nothing like the prestige and glamour of a long sitting. When you sit, you can feel and look like the Buddha or a great yogi. This has all the appearance of a 'spiritual' discipline, even if you're just falling asleep or worrying about money.

When you're eating, however, you're just eating, like everyone else. Nothing special at all, really. You can see why people dismiss the idea of spot-meditations. They seem like second-rate options for people who aren't serious.

Or are they? The reality is that relaxing a little many times a day is much more valuable than relaxing deeply just once. A long meditation is a wonderful and useful escape, like taking a holiday to Bali, but spot-meditating can keep you balanced and clear-minded in the midst of the turmoil. Moreover spot-meditations are actually possible in our complex lives. We can't wait for our next trip to Bali whenever we feel stressed.

Spot-meditating is unspectacular but the long-term effects are incalculable. If you eat with awareness, you're likely to eat less and enjoy it more, and to eat the food that is good for you. On the other hand, if you eat mechanically, you're more likely to be overweight and miserable.

If you walk consciously, you can walk with ease, shedding the tensions of the preceding minutes and enjoying the world around you. If you walk consumed in thought, however, you could be reinforcing the muscular rigidity of a lifetime.

If you relax a little whenever you can, you'll pace yourself well and feel you have the space and time to enjoy your life. Alternatively, if you push yourself relentlessly, you'll feel harassed and tired most of the time. Spot-meditations will soften the daily stresses and refresh your day much better than long meditations.

WHAT IS A SPOT-MEDITATION?

To make the idea of 'being here' come to life, it has to be done as a conscious exercise. You can't just think, 'be here', while you do the dishes and expect much satisfaction. This book will give you a huge range of spot-meditations to experiment with, but first let me explain what I mean by this term.

A spot-meditation is any meditation between ten seconds and ten minutes long, done under any circumstances. It is when you meditate 'on the spot'. Many of the exercises here are only a minute long, while some naturally stretch out to ten minutes or so. I call this book *The 5-Minute Meditator*, because five minutes is a good compromise length between short and long.

There are two main types of spot-meditations. With some, you relax rapidly for a short time – while in a waiting room or a queue for example – by giving them full attention. In other words, you stop what you are doing in order to meditate. The other kind is where you meditate while also doing something else. If you aim to be relaxed and aware while walking or doing housework, you can easily continue for several minutes.

BEYOND THIS BOOK

I've already written about spot-meditations in my major book, variously called *Do You Want to Meditate?* or *Teach Yourself to Meditate*, which has now sold 150,000 copies world-wide. Although other publishers produce my book overseas, I prefer to publish it myself in Australia. This gives me the freedom to revise it every three or four years to keep it abreast of my teaching style.

Since it is now time to give spot-meditations a book of their own, the next edition of *Do You Want to Meditate?* will allow me to focus on long meditations and the development of awareness. That book, the fully revised fifth edition of *Do You Want to Meditate?* will appear around January 2006.

If you want to pursue meditation further, you could aim to make your meditations longer, particularly those relating to the breath and the body. Probably the easiest way to do this is to use my set of CDs, called *How to Meditate*. This contains mostly long guided meditations with subtle musical accompaniment, and duplicates the way I teach in class.

1 minute
5 minutes ±
10 minutes

You could also develop your repertoire of spot-meditations. If you set yourself the goal of being relaxed and clear-minded in everything you do, that will keep you busy for a year or two.

I've always done spot-meditations, but in recent years they've become the cornerstone of my practice. Long meditations were always easy for me to do, but to be calm and clear-minded in the midst of an ordinary life was more of a challenge. Paradoxically this means that spot-meditations are both the entry level for new meditators – they're so easy to do – and they're also the graduate level, capable of endless subtleties and unexpected rewards. Spot-meditating is where you start, but it is also what skilled meditators do when they get off their cushions.

I love these rewarding little practices. They de-stress me rapidly and bring beauty and intelligence into my working day. Physical exercise keeps my body healthy; spot-meditations revitalise my soul. These modest and self-effacing practices can eventually give you results that are almost miraculous. I've seen them transform the lives of people who never do long meditations, and I know this can happen for you. I would love to see you pick up this skill and make it your own. Please try them out and be playful with them. Your imagination can be your own best guide. May you get as much satisfaction from them as I do.

Eric Harrison

www.perthmeditationcentre.com.au

Part One

Breath and Body

1

How To Use This Book

You'll find that spot-meditating is extraordinarily versatile once you get the knack of it. You don't need a special mantra or posture or a certain length of time or a quiet place. You certainly don't need yoga mats or soft music or a pure diet or a spiritual master. Instead you can relax and calm your mind virtually any time you are alone, and often in company also.

Yet despite this freedom, there is one absolute truth you can't get around: you only get good at a skill if you practise it. In this chapter I will explain how to get maximum benefit from the ideas in this book.

First of all, select your meditations: there are too many to do them all at once. I suggest you read this book with big pauses. When you find an exercise that appeals to you then put down the book and do it. Try to do it at least four times over four days, to establish it in long-term memory. Gradually develop a repertoire of exercises that you enjoy.

Key Words

Select your meditation
Find your time and place
Practise regularly

Secondly, find your time and place. Don't expect an opportunity to suddenly appear in front of you. Even if your day seems hopelessly busy, keep asking the question 'When could I meditate?' or 'Could I be more relaxed right now?' You'll soon find the opportunities if you look for them.

Thirdly, practise regularly. I suggest you aim for a minimum of ten minutes a day, five days a week, if you really want satisfaction. You don't have to sacrifice anything else to make the time, but you do need to be persistent if you want to convert 'being here' from an attractive idea into a reality. You'll find that ten minutes a day will soon pay for itself handsomely.

Finally, look for improvement, not perfection. Spot-meditating is about relaxing a little and often, not about going into states of ecstasy (though that happens too!). Don't expect to feel fully relaxed and calm after a two-minute meditation. Instead, just ask yourself 'Do I feel better than I did two minutes ago?'

THE STRUCTURE OF THE BOOK

Most of the chapters in this book introduce a meditation and give instructions on how to do it, while some chapters are purely explanatory. The next three chapters, for example, explain how meditation works, what relaxation actually is, and how to use the breath as biofeedback. These give you the context for the practical 'how to' chapters that follow.

Part One explains the meditations based on the breath and the body, which give you an excellent foundation for the more varied meditations that follow. You really can relax by focusing on a leaf or on a sandwich or while ironing clothes, but it still helps to be aware of your body while doing so.

Part Two explains how to relax by enhancing your sensual involvement with the world. Part Three gives you the exercises that the Buddha and I regard as essential if you really want to 'do what you're doing'. Part Four is a subsection on meditating while doing physical exercise. Part Five shows how to apply all of the above to various daily activities.

The 'how to' chapters mostly follow a three-part structure designed for maximum ease of use. Typically, a short introduction leads into the instructions, which are followed by a more lengthy commentary. The instructions are quite pithy – often just seven or eight lines long – to make them easy to remember when you actually do the exercise. The commentary gives further explanations, so you know what you're actually doing.

I suggest you read a chapter three or four times over a couple of days to get a good grasp of any particular exercise. Once you understand how to do it, you'll no longer need to reread the commentary. If you want to revise an exercise, you can go straight to those few lines of the instructions alone. In effect, you could tear out those pages and discard the rest of the book.

Part One   Breath and Body

5

Three Big Sighs

When we are tense, we breathe from the chest rather than the belly. We also tend to hold our breaths in, which makes our in-breaths longer than the rather truncated out-breaths. If you want to relax, the quickest way to reverse this is to sigh.

One of my students told me he was trying to persuade a high-flying executive friend to relax. "Just stop and take three deep breaths," he said. "Don't be silly," she wailed. "I haven't got the time!" If you have time to breathe, you have time to sigh.

Three Sighs is the most time-efficient meditation you will ever do. It's very short – maybe twenty seconds long – but you can change your state of body and mind markedly in that time. The slow, deep tempo of sighing is the perfect antidote to the fast, shallow, erratic pattern of tense breathing. The effect usually lingers for a few minutes afterwards, and when you find yourself starting to tense up, you can always sigh again.

Think of a sigh as having three parts: the in-breath, the out-breath and the pause at the end. The big in-breath opens the tight chest muscles. The out-breath is all about letting go control – you let the breath drop through the body without forcing it. Then you wait in the pause at the end for as long as is comfortable. Two or three big conscious sighs will break the pattern of tight breathing. If you want to continue relaxing thereafter, you can 'sigh gently' for a minute or two thereafter, as explained in the next chapter.

29

1. Three Sighs

Breathe in deeply, opening the ribcage.
Sigh: let the breath go without forcing it.
Rest in the pause, feeling the belly soften.
Wait until you really need to breathe in again.
Take a second big in-breath.
Feel the chest open further.
Drop into the soft, loose out-breath.
Pause again and wait.
And a third time, feeling everything loosen.
Let your breathing resume its natural rhythm.
It will now feel slow, deep and soft.
Breathe naturally or sigh gently as you wish.

COMMENTARY

Three Sighs is a classical spot-meditation: it's so versatile and portable that everyone should do regularly. It can be done anywhere, anytime, in any position or activity and with your eyes open or closed. It will get you out of your head and bring you back to earth immediately. Sigh as often as you feel like. You can easily do it twenty times a day. Don't worry if your family or workmates think you're unhappy or exasperated. To be relaxed is more important than what people think about you!

I commonly sigh whenever I stand up and start to walk somewhere – even if it's just across the room. When I get up from the computer, I deliberately sigh to open up my posture. Whenever I walk out of my house or get out of my car, I think 'Breathe!'

The big in-breath opens my chest and oxygenates my lungs. The long out-breath lets all the stale air go and softens the belly, and the pause at the end centres my mind in my body. I feel my posture become more upright and open and energised. Three Sighs are a delight, and well worth these few seconds!

KEY WORDS AND PHRASES

I know that people don't remember or even read all of what they find in a self-help book, and in fact it's not necessary. You'll get the most benefit if you pluck out the few ideas and exercises that appeal to you, and then develop them imaginatively.

To help you do this, I use a lot of extractable 'key words and phrases'. You can also think of them as instructions or affirmations or mantra or slogans or as seed-ideas. These words and phrases are often the actual titles of exercises: 'Sigh', 'Soften the body', 'Stop before you start'. They are also embedded in the instructions: 'Let the breath go', 'Focus on the active muscles', 'Just listen'. You'll also find them in the commentary to crystallise certain ideas: 'Do what you are doing', 'Be sensual', 'Just watch'.

I often put some of these words and phrases into a 'Key Words' box in the margin. I suggest you select ones you like and use them to steer your meditation. Once you get the idea, you can generate your own.

SAY, CHANT OR THINK THE WORD

There are three main ways you can use any of these phrases: as a trigger or as a chant or as a guiding principle. In the first case, you would mentally say the phrase just once to initiate the action: 'Breathe out and stop' or 'Soften the body'. This will give you a strong, clear start to the exercise.

Secondly, you would say a phrase repeatedly like an inner chant. For example, you could silently say 'let go' each time you breathe, saying the first word as you breathe in and the second as you breathe out. This has a slightly hypnotic, soothing effect and occupies the mind well, helping to marginalise your usual mental chatter. Don't try to chant in a regular, musical fashion, however. Make sure the words follow your natural breathing, which is usually somewhat irregular. If a breath is long, then lengthen the words. If it is short, then shorten them.

Thirdly, you could gently hold the concept in your mind as a reference point throughout the exercise. If you think 'Do what you're doing' or 'Be sensual' while you do the dishes, you'll soon notice when your mind is somewhere else entirely.

If you want, you can also contemplate the meaning of a word, but don't overdo it. Remember that the feeling behind the word is much more important than the word itself. If you think 'When walking, just walk', it reminds you what to do: focus on your body and your breath to feel yourself relaxing. Let the past and future and all their problems slip into the background for a while.

Or you could think the phrase 'Be sensual'. Tune into sight, sound, smell, taste or touch. Wind down from the electric speed of thought to the earthiness of physical sensation. Notice when you're slipping back into thought or daydreaming.

So let me briefly summarise the above. There are three main ways to use key words and phrases:

1. Say the word once to initiate an action.
2. Silently chant a word or phrase with the breath.
3. Think about the word as a guiding principle.

In other words, you could either say, chant or think the word.

Over time, these words can become surprisingly potent for you. They can help you evoke a certain feeling and remind you what you're aiming for. You gradually convert a concept into a fully grounded experience. When you say the word 'Peace', you will know what it feels like in your body.

Once you understand a certain phrase or instruction, you can abbreviate it to a single word. For example you could reduce 'Breathe out and stop before you start' to just 'Breathe!' or 'Stop', and you'll find that the single word will still carry the full meaning of the phrase within it.

This book has some forty-five thousand words in it. I would be very happy if you took from it just ten or twelve key words and phrases, and three or four exercises you felt confident with. If you worked with these imaginatively, that could be all you need.

2

How To Calm The Mind

Meditation can seem very complicated. People variously meditate to relax, to heal cancer, to think more clearly, to find their inner selves, to play better tennis, to get rich or to fall asleep! Meditation also comes in many flavours – Hindu, Buddhist, Christian and New Age – and frequently promises heaven and earth.

Yet most practices are very similar beneath the surface. You could say they are a thousand different expressions of the same underlying principles. We can define meditation as 'any practice that relaxes the body quickly and calms the mind.'

In fact, body and mind are so closely connected you can regard them as one organism. As a result, you could relax either the body or the mind for the whole system to relax. Yoga, massage and warm baths are all ways of relaxing the body. Meditation on the other hand calms the mind, which thereby relaxes the body as well.

THE OVERACTIVE MIND

Why is it so hard to calm the mind? For most of us, our minds never seem to settle down. We get swamped by an endless stream of hopes, worries, plans and inner dialogues. Of course, we all have to think but most of us think too much. To relax at all, we need to weaken the habit of incessant thought.

It is actually the emotional charge behind our thoughts that stirs us up. Worry may be driving our thoughts about work. Anger or irritation may underpin our thoughts about family. Desire may be driving our planning for the weekend. None of these emotions is inherently bad but they definitely stop us relaxing.

These emotions pump out adrenalin, which stimulates the nervous system into some degree of the fight-or-flight response. Adrenalin sends signals throughout the body saying, 'Prepare for action! We've got to sort this thing out. This is no time to relax.' Thinking is not just a head trip: it reverberates through your whole body.

Thinking is like putting fuel on a fire. An overactive mind literally fires us up. Adrenalin raises our stress response and makes us burn energy fast. You could be trying to relax by doing nothing on a pleasant Sunday afternoon, but if your mind is overactive you'll still feel stressed. A bricklayer, 'just doing what he is doing', would be more relaxed.

Unfortunately, we do have a lot to think about. We face the ongoing demands of work, relationships, maintaining health and preparing for the future in an accelerating world. We even face a bewildering excess of *good* things: so much we can do and see and buy every day. These stimulate the flow of adrenalin in much the same way that worry does.

Furthermore, we often feel deeply troubled beneath the surface of our busy lives. Despite our optimistic hopes, we know we're trying to find happiness in a dangerous and irrational world. The pain and mistakes of our past will still echo through us. We know that sickness, misery and death are all around, and they creep closer to us as we age. We feel the rapid degradation of the planet, and the avarice and arrogance of the people in power. This dark undercurrent of thought and feeling can make us perpetually on edge and afraid to relax at all.

thoughts +

emotion →

adrenalin →

more thoughts

TOO MUCH THOUGHT IS TOXIC

Thinking promises to give us solutions, but in fact the more we think the worse we think. Thinking stimulates our nervous system, but it also exhausts us since we burn through our reserves fast. Nearly a third of our body's daily energy expenditure occurs in our brain. A tired, over-stimulated mind is easily distracted and can't follow a line of thought coherently. Our minds fixate on small things and we lose all sense of proportion. We react to a red light or a lost sock as if our world is collapsing.

Eventually you become tired enough to fall asleep at night, but the thinking doesn't stop just because you're unconscious of it. If you wake someone from sleep, they can tell you exactly what they were thinking about. Chronic thinking can wreck the quality of our sleep for years. In time, it can be as damaging for our health as chronic smoking or drinking.

Meditation lets us choose when and how much we think. We don't try to ignore our problems. We just don't dwell on them more than necessary. We do have some control about how we react to the stressors around us. Some people fret to death over a broken fingernail. Others can be peaceful in a war zone or a refugee camp.

We don't have to fume at the red light: we could breathe gently and wait. We could be seriously ill, but it doesn't help to panic about it as well. Work pressures could be huge, but you don't need to think about them twenty-four hours a day. In the worst of times, you can still find moments of beauty and love. Meditation lets you be as calm and clear-minded as is possible in any situation.

HOW DOES MEDITATION WORK?

To relax at all, we have to weaken the habit of incessant thought. Usually when our thoughts irritate us, we try to block them out or finish them off, but neither option works well. Trying to block thoughts takes effort and makes you tense, and every thought comes with a hook leading to the next thought. We need more subtle options.

Meditation gives us two distinct ways of cooling down the overactive mind. These are called 'focusing' and 'awareness'. Focusing is obvious and effective, and it may be all you need for the spot-meditations in this book. It is the heavy engine that drives meditation. Awareness is more subtle but let me briefly describe it first.

We can't avoid noticing a thought that appears in the mind, but we don't have to engage it in conversation. We can simply notice it and let go our grip on it. The thought may then fade or remain, but either way we don't throw fuel on the fire. We call this the art of 'just watching', or 'being an observer', or 'pure awareness'. In time, you'll find you can step back from all your thoughts and feelings and simply 'watch them with detachment'. You can let the stream of consciousness flow by you while you watch from the bank.

'Just watching' your thoughts might sound easy in principle, but the mind is reluctant to be so passive. Even a calm mind is naturally curious and the stream of consciousness is full of 'important' things to deal with. In order to divert us from the temptations of thought, and in lieu of doing nothing (which is impossible), we do something as simple as possible: we focus on just one thing or one activity to the exclusion of all else.

FOCUSING SHIFTS YOU FROM THINKING TO SENSING

In particular, meditation asks you to focus on the sensations of the present – sight, sound, smell, taste or touch. If you focus on the breath, or on the sounds around you, or on the food you are eating, you marginalise the thoughts relating to the past and future. Your blood-flow literally drains away from those parts of the brain involved in cerebral thought. You enhance your sensory awareness at the expense of thinking.

While you try to 'be here', your mind will often detour back to thinking, but even intermittent focus on a sensual object will relax you. By focusing, you hold one thing in the foreground, while letting your habitual thoughts burble along unattended in the background. Those thoughts won't die but they become weaker and less troublesome. If you don't feed them, they don't stimulate a stress response.

There is nothing imaginary about this mental shift from thinking mode to sensing mode. You can read the shift on an electroencephalograph after just twenty seconds of sustained sensing. Thinking produces 'beta' brain waves, which are fast, erratic and of low amplitude. Sensing produces 'alpha' brain waves which are slower, rhythmic and of high amplitude. Something very real is happening in your biochemistry.

Subjectively we feel that shift in other ways. Thinking is busy and active, involving concepts of past and future. It is usually powered by some variant of fear, anger or desire. It is a high–energy state, exciting but also exhausting. Your body will be tense and you will tend to hold your breath.

Sensing is quite the opposite. It is more passive and keeps you in the present. It is emotionally looser, burns less energy and feels more sustainable. It is relaxing and more pleasant. Your body will be soft and your breathing loose.

Thinking:	Sensing:
is active	is more passive
involves past and future	is in the present
is complex and fast	is simpler and slower
has high emotional charge	has low emotional charge
is stimulating	is relaxing
burns energy	conserves energy
tightens the body	lets the body soften

GOOD FOCUS IS THE KEY

The basic meditation strategy - focus on something sensual and let the thoughts go - is relatively clear, but it needs practice. Doing something sensual is not the same as focusing on it. We can easily eat a peach without tasting it at all. The mind is very fast and could be anywhere.

Focusing means paying careful attention to one thing. When eating a peach, you feel your teeth breaking the skin, the juice on your tongue and saliva flowing. You notice how fresh it is, you savour the mixture of taste and smell, and even hear the sounds you make as you eat.

When you focus well on breathing, for example, you actually feel your body expand and contract. You follow each breath to the end and catch that little pause before the in-breath starts. You enjoy the gentle ebb and flow of the breath as it massages your body from inside. This is good focus. You bring the moment-to-moment sensations of the breath into focus, like focusing a camera.

Your mind becomes slower when you focus well. Sensing slows us down from the volatility of thought to the immediacy of just feeling, just seeing, just hearing. When busy, your mind can easily speed at the rate of three or four thoughts a second all day long. If, on the other hand, you focus on just one sensation or activity for even fifteen seconds, you slow down the speed of the mind enormously. Focusing the mind is like tying a horse to a post, as the old texts say.

Some meditators have trouble with the idea of focus, associating it with knitted brows and grim determination. They confuse relaxation with sleepiness. They feel that you shouldn't focus at all but just 'let everything go' and gradually space out. In meditation, however, you focus quite gently. You use just a little effort to stay on track but you don't need to force it.

Focusing is completely natural and we do it every day. It occurs whenever something attracts our attention – a flowering bush, a snatch of music, a beautiful body walking by. A child absorbed in a toy is focused, sensing and present.

Everyone can focus to some degree. You couldn't get home without it. Meditation just enhances this natural ability. Eventually we want to focus because the results are so satisfying. When you focus well, the body relaxes rapidly and the mind becomes clear and still. You don't get that effect if you just space out and drift away.

Key Words

Be here

Focus on the sensations of the present

Shift from thinking to sensing

Let thoughts go

Just watch

Focusing is the simplest way to divert your mind from thought and to 'be present'. The only major difference between meditations is what you focus on. In the exercises to come, I'll ask you to focus in many ways on the breath, the body, sights, sounds, tastes and various activities. These all work on the same principles: if you consciously focus on the sensations of the present, and disengage from your habitual thoughts, you automatically relax.

3

Relaxation And The Body

Meditation, despite its spiritual connotations, is solidly based on the relaxation of the body. If your body doesn't relax, your meditation remains a head-trip and nothing much happens. Some meditation practices, such as visualisation and mantra and positive thinking, virtually ignore the body or take it for granted, but they are a bit weak and ungrounded as a result. In fact, you relax best if you're highly attuned to your body.

Paradoxically, the fastest way to relax is to notice how tense you are. Once you realise that you're holding your breath and that your shoulders are high, you don't even have to think what to do next: you automatically breathe out and drop your shoulders. This is how awareness acts as biofeedback, telling you where and when you're tense and what to do about it.

Awareness reminds you that it's your choice whether to hold on (to be tense) or to let go (to relax). You don't actually have to 'do' anything other than let go the unnecessary tension, but you do have to be aware of it in the first place. It stands to reason that the more you can read your body, the more skilfully you can let go.

For example, if you check your breathing, you'll soon know how tense or relaxed you are. Tense breathing is tight and arrhythmic, and comes from the chest. Relaxed breathing on the other hand is loose, deep and flowing. Similarly, when you're tense, your muscles feel hard and jumpy. When you relax, they feel soft and warm.

As you develop more rapport with your body, the payoff can be enormous. You can easily relax your breathing with a few conscious sighs, and soften your face and shoulders within seconds. If you're not conscious of these tensions, or are ignoring them, they can remain tight all your life (I'm not exaggerating).

THE BIOLOGY OF RELAXATION

We usually think of tension and relaxation as states of mind, but in fact they are embedded in the body. They are the sympathetic and parasympathetic responses of the central nervous system. Tension is the 'fight or flight' response that turns on adrenalin and cortisone, giving us the energy we need to face the demands of the day. Relaxation is the reverse process that turns off the stress hormones, letting us return to balance and eventually taking us to sleep. Meditation, therefore, turns off the 'stress response' and turns on the 'relaxation response'.

In fact, your adrenalin levels govern both responses. High adrenalin levels stimulate you and as the adrenalin fades, you automatically relax. It's like using the accelerator pedal in a car to go faster or slower. You press it down when you want to burn more fuel, and you ease up when you want to go slower or stop.

In other words, we use adrenalin to tense up or relax during the day according to how much energy we feel we need at any time. This is just the way our nervous system works: it naturally oscillates between arousal and relaxation all day long. At any time, you're either speeding up or slowing down – you're either burning energy or conserving it.

When you're stressed, you're 'speedy' and you burn energy fast: you push the pedal flat to the floor. That's when you race around, go nowhere fast and often crash. When you relax, on the other hand, you slow down and conserve energy. You can still be active and efficient, but you're in cruise mode. We are all good at speeding up – we can raise our stress levels in a flash. But hardly any of us are good at relaxing. That is a different matter altogether.

BEING IN BALANCE: THE IDEAL OPERATING ZONE

Some activities – sleeping, sitting and listening, for example – require little energy, while other activities need much more. However, there is a 'right' amount of energy expenditure for any particular activity – not too much and not too little. If your energy levels are in tune with what you are doing, you can say you're 'in balance'.

AROUSAL		
100%	Panic	
	Stress	
	Balance	
	Relaxation	
0%	Sleep	

It is possible to be reasonably balanced all day long. Your energy expenditure will vary according to what you do, but it can always be 'right' for that particular task.

Mild Daily Oscillations: Balance

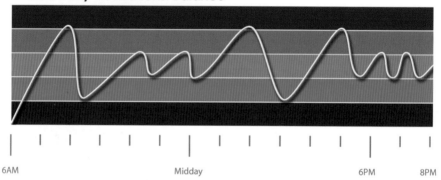

6AM   Midday   6PM   8PM

Big Daily Oscillations: Stress

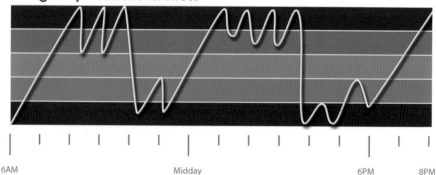

6AM   Midday   6PM   8PM

Ideally, your nervous system should oscillate between mild arousal and mild relaxation all day long, and avoid the extremes of panic and exhaustion. It's all a matter of pacing yourself well, relaxing when you can and being attuned to what you are doing.

This idea is encapsulated in the Buddhist saying 'When walking, just walk'. If you *worry* while you walk, however, you'll burn more energy than 'just walking' requires. The stress hormones will make everything pump and squeeze and race harder in the body – far more than you need for 'just walking'. If you overreact to every problem, and fret about them for too long, you could be way out of balance. You could be burning 50% more energy than necessary for every activity all day long.

If you burn energy fast, you eventually burn out. The body will compensate by throwing you into a state of exhaustion, which forces you to rest whether you like it or not. This is the familiar stress–fatigue cycle. We push too hard when we've got some energy (or coffee) inside us, and then struggle with fatigue the rest of the time.

If you imagine this pattern stretched over a lifetime you can see why years of anxiety (the high energy state) are often followed by years of depression (the low energy state). A common pattern is to be bright and bubbly in your twenties, perpetually anxious in your thirties, and sick and depressed in your forties. Trying to live on adrenalin can destroy you.

Key Words
Be aware of stress
Let go the breath
Soften the body
When walking, just walk
Be in balance
Relax a little and often

The sad end of an adrenalin junky

RELAX A LITTLE AND OFTEN

By spot-meditating, you can consciously return to balance whenever you need to. Since prolonged stress is physically painful, the body has a strong instinct to escape it. All it needs is a little encouragement. If you stop what you're doing, take a few deep breaths and sigh, you can relax markedly in less than a minute. You'll also stay relaxed and burn less energy in the minutes that follow.

You don't have to relax deeply for a meditation to be worthwhile. To relax just 20% many times a day is enormously valuable. It can rescue you from the horrors of a panic attack. If you're running about frantically, you can cool down in a minute or two. If you're overreacting to something, you can stop immediately. If you need to rest, you can quickly sink into a catnap, sitting in your car in the car park. If you're jumping out of your skin with boredom at a meeting, you can zone out while still appearing to be there.

Alternatively, you may find that you're a persistent worrier for no good reason, and it stops you enjoying life. Even if prolonged stress in the past has trained you to be hyper-vigilant, a spot-meditation can still work its magic. It can easily disarm your worry, and take you into a world of momentary stillness and beauty. You can find that within your adult body you still have the eyes of a child (a happy one!)

Few of us can do long meditations as often as we would like. Half an hour a day would be a great achievement and sacrifice for most people. If you learn to spot-meditate, however, you could easily be relaxed and calm for several hours a day, without disturbing your usual activities. In fact it is likely to enhance them.

In time you can retrain your body's responses. You don't have to habitually gulp your food or walk stiffly or talk as if your life depended on it. It's much more pleasant to actually taste your food, and to breathe while you walk. Being present immediately increases the sensual pleasure of living. By repeatedly switching off the stress response with spot-meditations, you can train yourself to be in a healthy, balanced state for most of the day. The secret is to keep listening to your body.

4

Use Your Breath To Relax

The quickest way to relax is to use your breath. In fact, a single deep breath will start to loosen you up if you're tense. Since the body and mind are one organism, if you consciously relax your breathing, your mind will calm down also. In the chapters ahead, I'll suggest three different ways you can use the breath. They are:

1. Sighing
2. Relaxed Breathing
3. Deep Breathing

We all do the first two naturally. They require no effort or skill, but I'd like you to do them more consciously and often. These are all you need for most of the spot-meditations in this book.

The third one, 'Deep Breathing' is simple enough, but it asks you to tune into the mechanism of breathing in more detail. Some people find this easy to do, but for others it is more effort than it is worth.

The next four chapters explain sighing and relaxed breathing. The following three chapters integrate the breath with body awareness. The remaining chapters in Part One explain Deep Breathing, how to relax while walking and how to do a long breath meditation.

HOW TO RECOGNISE TENSE AND RELAXED BREATHING

The way we breathe at any time perfectly mirrors our mental and physical state. We breathe a certain way when we're tense and worried, and quite differently when we're relaxed and happy. The breath is always giving us useful feedback on how tense or relaxed we are, if we choose to listen to it.

So what is tense breathing? Virtually everyone when they're anxious breathes in the same way. You breathe from the chest, not the belly. The chest muscles are tight and you hold the breath in, which makes the in-breaths longer than the out-breaths. Holding the breath also stops its natural rhythm, so the movement is jerky and tight.

Relaxed breathing is the opposite. You breathe from lower in the body, if not from the belly itself. You let the breath go, so the out-breaths become longer than the in-breaths. The breathing becomes softer, looser and more flowing. There is often a momentary pause at the end of the out-breath where everything goes still. This is the complete opposite of tense breathing, where you hold at the top of the in-breath.

Tense Breathing	Relaxed Breathing
From the chest	From the belly
Longer in-breaths	Longer out-breaths
(Holding at the top)	(Resting at the bottom)
Tight and jerky	Soft and flowing

Let me briefly explain how the three meditations above help you relax the breath, and therefore the body and mind as well. You'll find more complete instructions in the chapters that follow.

THE SIGH

The fastest way to start relaxing is to consciously sigh. It reverses almost all the signs of tense breathing listed above. The big in-breath opens the tight chest muscles. The sigh itself makes the out-breath longer than the in-breath. And after two or three big sighs, you'll find yourself breathing in from deeper in the body. The sigh also breaks that 'holding at the top' of the breath that occurs when you're tense.

Two or three big sighs is a meditation all of its own (see Chapter 5), but you can't go on sighing like that without hyperventilating. Thereafter you can either 'Sigh Gently' with minimal effort (Chapter 6), or shift into 'Relaxed Breathing' (Chapter 7).

RELAXED BREATHING

Relaxed breathing is not a breathing exercise: it is just the natural, uncontrolled way you breathe when you are relaxed. However, by simply focusing on the breathing and 'letting go' the out-breath, you will find the breath relaxes automatically and the body and mind follow.

The defining feature of relaxed breathing is that the out-breaths are longer than the in-breaths. Relaxed breathing is not necessarily deep or rhythmic or what you may think of as good breathing. It can be somewhat erratic, with the odd sigh and short catch-up breaths thrown in. It naturally changes according to your state of mind and the activity you're engaged it. A relaxed breath is just relaxed: the out-breath is longer than the in-breath. That's all you need to look for.

DEEP, RELAXED BREATHING

Deep breathing is not hard to do, but it is more of a physical exercise than the above. Deep breathing, as I explain it, literally means 'breathing from deep in the body'. Because you use your belly and diaphragm *at the expense of* the upper chest muscles, deep breathing is an antidote to the chest breathing that goes with anxiety. It is also different from 'full breathing', as you find in Yoga, which uses the whole breathing mechanism.

A deep breath still needs to be a relaxed breath, in the sense that the out-breath is longer than the in-breath. In fact, Deep, Relaxed Breathing can be almost the same as 'Sighing Gently'. Sighs naturally come from deep in the body, and the long loose out-breath when you sigh is much the same as that of a relaxed, deep breath. A 'deep' breath has a little more effort on the in-breath but the difference is minimal. Deep Breathing and Sighing Gently suit those spot-meditations in which you are walking or otherwise being physically active.

Key Words

When tense, you hold on
When relaxed, you let go

5

Three Big Sighs

hen we are tense, we breathe from the chest rather than the belly. We also tend to hold our breaths in, which makes our in-breaths longer than the rather truncated out-breaths. If you want to relax, the quickest way to reverse this is to sigh.

One of my students told me he was trying to persuade a high-flying executive friend to relax. "Just stop and take three deep breaths," he said. "Don't be silly," she wailed. "I haven't got the time!" If you have time to breathe, you have time to sigh.

Three Sighs is the most time-efficient meditation you will ever do. It's very short – maybe twenty seconds long – but you can change your state of body and mind markedly in that time. The slow, deep tempo of sighing is the perfect antidote to the fast, shallow, erratic pattern of tense breathing. The effect usually lingers for a few minutes afterwards, and when you find yourself starting to tense up, you can always sigh again.

Think of a sigh as having three parts: the in-breath, the out-breath and the pause at the end. The big in-breath opens the tight chest muscles. The out-breath is all about letting go control – you let the breath drop through the body without forcing it. Then you wait in the pause at the end for as long as is comfortable. Two or three big conscious sighs will break the pattern of tight breathing. If you want to continue relaxing thereafter, you can 'sigh gently' for a minute or two, as explained in the next chapter.

1. Three Sighs

Breathe in deeply, opening the ribcage.

Sigh: let the breath go without forcing it.

Rest in the pause, feeling the belly soften.

Wait until you really need to breathe in again.

Take a second big in-breath.

Feel the chest open further.

Drop into the soft, loose out-breath.

Pause again and wait.

And a third time, feeling everything loosen.

Let your breathing resume its natural rhythm.

It will now feel slow, deep and soft.

Breathe naturally or sigh gently as you wish.

COMMENTARY

Three Sighs is a classical spot-meditation: it's so versatile and portable that everyone should do it regularly. It can be done anywhere, anytime, in any position or activity and with your eyes open or closed. It will get you out of your head and bring you back to earth immediately. Sigh as often as you feel like. You can easily do it twenty times a day. Don't worry if your family or workmates think you're unhappy or exasperated. To be relaxed is more important than what people think about you!

I commonly sigh whenever I stand up and start to walk somewhere – even if it's just across the room. When I get up from the computer, I deliberately sigh to open up my posture. Whenever I walk out of my house or get out of my car, I think 'Breathe!'

The big in-breath opens my chest and oxygenates my lungs. The long out-breath lets all the stale air go and softens the belly, and the pause at the end centres my mind in my body. I feel my posture become more upright and open and energised. Three Sighs are a delight, and well worth those few seconds!

WHY THE SIGH WORKS SO WELL

Let's now look in more detail at those three parts of the sigh: the in-breath, the out-breath and the pause.

When you're tense, the upper chest and neck muscles are bound to be tight. That's virtually the signature sensation of anxiety. However the first part of a sigh – the big in-breath – stretches and opens up those muscles. Tight muscles often won't relax unless you stretch them out first, and you need more than one breath to do that. That is why you consciously take those big in-breaths. If you sigh while keeping the chest muscles tight, it won't be anywhere near as effective.

When you sigh, just let the breath drop as far as it wants to go without forcing it. If you're quite tense, don't be surprised if it doesn't go very far. When your muscles are tight, they naturally hold the breath in and up. After two or three big in-breaths however, you'll find there's more room in the ribcage and the out-breaths will drop deeper each time.

A genuine sigh has a pause at the end, where everything stops for a few seconds. It doesn't hurry through to the next in-breath. If there wasn't a pause, it wouldn't be a sigh at all – it would just be a deep breath. That pause can be surprisingly long and peaceful: no breath and usually no thoughts either. I suggest you just wait there, listening for that inner voice that says 'You need to breathe in again now.'

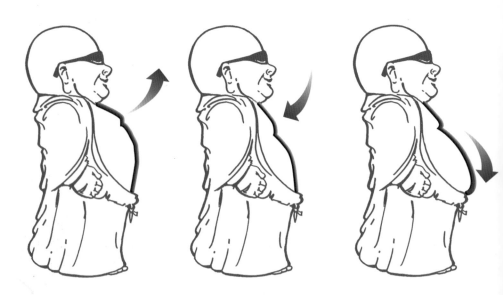

ADD A YAWN

Sighs and yawns happen naturally when you're relaxing, or about to relax, and they only occur when you let go some unconscious preoccupation in the mind. It is as if you instinctively realise the crisis is over and it's safe to release the tension in a sigh. By consciously sighing, you send a signal from your body back to the mind, saying 'It's okay to relax now. See? I'm sighing.'

A yawn is a kind of turbocharged sigh. If you also yawn as you sigh, you get maximum payoff from your few seconds of meditation. Firstly, a yawn refreshes you by increasing oxygen intake. More importantly, it stretches the powerful jaw muscles that many people clench tight all day (and often all night, grinding their teeth in their sleep). A yawn doesn't just loosen the breathing: it also releases the jaw, the eyes and temples and the connecting neck and shoulder muscles. Try it out and see.

I call this exercise 'Three Sighs' as three is a good number to aim for, but it is your choice how many sighs you take. Generally, if you take a huge sigh with an added yawn, you can only do one or two comfortably, whereas smaller sighs can continue for much longer.

In time, you will refine your sighs to suit your situation. You can take big sighs or small sighs. You can have discreet ladylike sighs when you are in company, and noisy open-mouthed sighs when you are alone. In general, big sighs are best when you stand or walk, and gentle sighs when you sit.

SIGH WELL

Simple and natural as a sigh is, you can still sigh badly! There are full, satisfying sighs that really work, and mediocre, half-hearted sighs that fail to make any impact on the onslaught of thoughts. The bigger the in-breath and the looser the out-breath, the better it works.

Key Words

Big in-breath

Yawn

Long out-breath

Let go

Pause

So give the sighs full attention for those twenty or so seconds. Don't sigh mechanically with your mind elsewhere and expect it to work. Feel the chest open more with each in-breath. Feel yourself release more with each out-breath. Enjoy the pause.

Above all, don't force the out-breath. A sigh is all about letting go control, so if you try too hard to make it happen, you'll miss the point. Don't try to artificially hold on to the pause at the end, either. Be relaxed about it! Let the new in-breath come when it wants to.

A perfectly executed sigh is just as elegant and satisfying, in its own small way, as a beautiful tennis stroke. If you focus fully on the sigh, your body and mind become one. The in-breath is full and expansive; the out-breath is luxurious and total, and the pause at the end seems to last forever. I hope you can become very good at sighing. Like a tennis stroke, it improves with daily practice.

6

Sigh Gently

The Three Sighs exercise is a circuit-breaker: you stop what you are doing and deliberately relax for a few seconds. If you want to continue relaxing however, you change from 'big' sighs to 'gentle' sighs. You sigh gently while doing housework, walking to the shops, waiting in traffic, working at the computer…

A 'gentle' sigh differs from a 'big' sigh in that you don't take those big energetic in-breaths. You simply focus on 'letting go' as you breathe out, feeling the breath become soft and loose, and you don't force the in-breath. You put no effort into a 'gentle' sigh other than the effort to let go.

Three Sighs quickly brings you to a halt, but you don't have to completely stop what you are doing in order to relax. You simply have to keep your breathing loose. Sigh gently while you do the dishes or hang out the washing or walk to the car. Of course, you're also bound to notice many thoughts and sensations other than the breath, but this doesn't matter. If you can keep just 20% of your attention on the breath, you'll soon find you do the dishes in a more relaxed and efficient manner.

Can you sigh gently while getting dressed, preparing a meal, sitting in a bus, walking to the shops, doing the paperwork or answering the phone? Your mind has to slow down somewhat to come into the present and actually notice the breath, but it's not that hard to do. If you have bursts of sighing throughout the day, you'll soon find you can de-stress rapidly whenever you want to.

You'll find that by letting the breath go you also let the troublesome thoughts go. It seems that we need a certain 'up' charge in the body for energetic thought which we get by holding our breaths. Conversely, you'll find your thoughts fade, or at least lose their intensity, in that soft, loose pause at the end of a sigh. As soon as you starting thinking again, notice how you immediately revert to holding your breath. Time for another sigh!

A single sigh is enough to coax you away from your habitual thoughts and into the present, and further sighs will keep you there. I suggest you start this exercise by sighing gently for the space of a five-minute walk. Try it out and notice how different you feel.

2. Sigh Gently

Take two or three big sighs.

Feel your body open up.

Now sigh gently for as long as you like.

Let go the out-breath fully.

Enjoy that moment of stillness at the end.

Let the in-breath come when it wants to: no effort.

Keep the breathing soft and loose.

Sigh gently while you continue with what you are doing.

7

Relaxed, Uncontrolled Breathing

If you are tense, the signs may be quite obvious: a rigid body, anxious mind, aching shoulders and knotted stomach. However, the clearest sign of all is how you breathe: you'll be unconsciously holding your breath in and breathing from the upper chest.

Adrenalin makes all the muscles in the body tight, and we grip on to the breath without realising it. Once you become aware of this holding on, however, it's easy to release it. Awareness can act like the touch of a magic wand, loosening the unconscious tensions that stop the release of the out-breath.

When you are relaxed, you'll find that you let the breath go, and the out-breath becomes longer than the in-breath. This is true whether you are half asleep or climbing a mountain. If you are just 'doing what you are doing' in a relaxed fashion, your out-breath will be longer than your in-breath. Check it out and see. This is the signature of relaxed breathing.

This meditation still goes through stages. After a few big sighs, and then a few gentle sighs, you gradually settle into relaxed, uncontrolled breathing. You'll find that as your breathing loosens up, your face, shoulders and belly will also soften in sympathy. You can do this exercise for just two or three minutes, or you could stretch it into a long meditation as explained in Chapter 15.

The mere fact that you are focusing on the sensations of the body, and diverting your attention from your habitual thoughts, is quite enough to relax you. Soon the pleasure principle takes over. You feel your body and breath continuing to relax, and your mind goes inwards, leaving the outer world and all its concerns behind. What a relief!

Relaxation is all about letting go. You let go the breath, your thoughts, and even the effort to relax. You can reinforce this idea by saying an affirmation as you breathe, like a silent chant. I suggest you say the words 'let go' repeatedly — saying the word 'let' on the in-breath, and 'go' on the out-breath.

3. Relaxed Breathing

Take two or three big sighs to open up the chest.

Then sigh gently for a little while.

Now let the breath go. No control at all.

Don't try to breathe deeply.

Don't hold the pause at the end, if there is one.

Let the breath do what it wants to.

Say the words 'let . . . go . . .' as you breathe.

Feel the breath gradually soften.

Feel your body softening.

Feel your mind slow down and settle in your body.

Keep the out-breath loose, whether you are sitting still or active.

COMMENTARY

THE ART OF LETTING GO

Whenever you meditate, it is good to use key words to remind you what to do. These are not essential but they can help more than you would expect. For this meditation, I suggest you say or think the affirmation 'let go', as you breathe, or you could use the words 'slow down' or 'relax'.

This will have the repetitive familiarity of a chant, and remind you what to look for. Make sure the words follow your natural breathing, however. If a breath is long, then stretch out the words. If it's short, then shorten them.

Relaxed breathing means you let go all attempts at control. Rest in that pause at the end of the breath, and don't hurry the in-breath. Let each breath have its little peculiarities. Don't try to make the breaths even, or to eliminate the 'catch-up' breaths. You don't try to breathe deeply or to sigh. Don't even try to make the out-breaths progressively longer – just a little longer than the in-breath will do fine. You're aiming for something that is so ordinary that we barely notice it: relaxed, uncontrolled breathing.

Relaxed breathing has a beautiful, sensual quality about it. It ebbs and flows within you and massages the body from inside. Eventually, you let everything go as you breathe out – the breath, muscle tension, thoughts and worries – and enjoy the supreme laziness of it all.

Meditators eventually discover this wonderful truth: you don't have to make yourself relax. You just stand back and let it happen. Focusing is just a device to distract you from your usual mental busyness, so you do less than usual.

Meditation in fact is the art of doing nothing. It is a kind of deliberate 'non-doing' and 'non-thinking'. The less you try to do, the better it works! The body has a profound instinct for what is healthy and comfortable. It knows exactly how it wants to breathe, and it will unerringly move that way if you give it half a chance.

Key Words
Let go (said as a chant)
Relax the breath
Soften the body
Do nothing

In fact, letting go and doing nothing is easier said than done. It's not in our character to do nothing at all. We want to think about something at least. Even if you're sitting still, the tight muscles within you could be working hard to stay tense, burning lots of energy and wearing you out. They are like sentries that can fall asleep while standing up, still holding their rifles.

So 'letting go and doing nothing' actually does involve doing something: you become more aware of your body. You notice the unnecessary tensions in the face, shoulders and stomach, and invite them to let go. In particular, you notice the hidden tensions that stop the release of the out-breath. 'The war is over', you say. 'It really is safe to breathe out now.'

We usually feel we have to 'do' something to relax, but in fact the opposite is true. We simply notice when the body and mind are toiling away unnecessarily and invite them to stop.

Relax, let go, trust…

8

Stop Before You Start

Anxious people typically can't stop at all. Their minds race and their bodies are perpetually restless, whether they're active or not. The fight-or-flight syndrome keeps them continually on the move or primed to move. When they do stop, they typically collapse into exhaustion, which is hardly a graceful way to land. From the moment they wake up they are on the run, until they hit their pillows at night.

It doesn't have to be this way. All of us have the chance to slow down and come to a halt maybe a hundred times a day, if only for a few seconds at a time. It is wonderful to be able to consciously stop one activity and then consciously start the next. This may seem impossible if you are habituated to speed, but it simply takes a little practice and understanding.

So look for the opportunities. Breathe out and stop before you answer the phone. Before you open the door. Before you drive away. Before you start your golf swing. Before you do the dishes. One full breath can be quite enough to create a punctuation mark before the next action. This exercise in fact abbreviates the Three Sighs meditation into a single sigh, and you get a very good return for your few seconds' investment.

I suggest you silently say a word or phrase to yourself to trigger the exercise. The full instructions for the below can be contained in the phrase: 'Breathe out and stop before you start'. Once you understand this exercise, you can abbreviate that phrase to suit yourself. Have a look at the options in the Key Words box.

4. Stop before you start

Before you start a new activity,

take a big breath and sigh.

Breathe out and mentally stop.

Find that point of stillness at the end of the breath.

Prepare yourself to act.

Consciously start the new action.

COMMENTARY

There is often a brief moment between one activity and another in which you can consciously stop, if you wish. If the phone rings, you don't have to instantly pick it up. You can pause and breathe out. You let the previous activity go and reorient yourself to the new task. Give yourself time to complete your one big sigh. Let the phone ring two or three times before you answer it. You'll be in a much better mental space when you do.

Just stop. Then start. Consciously pause between activities to make sure that you do stop. Breathe out and let the former activity go. Then start the next action deliberately and smoothly. It may surprise you to realise how ancient these instructions are. 'Notice how activities start and finish,' said the Buddha. ('And sensations and thoughts and feelings.')

You can completely stop in the space of a single breath, but don't confuse 'stopping' with 'freezing.' Feel the big in-breath open the tight chest muscles, and when you breathe out, let everything go. Wait in the pause until your body feels soft and still, and your mind feels centred in your body. Only then do you start the next activity.

Trivial as it seems, this can completely change the flavour of our day. When we're mentally restless, our minds leap ahead or lag behind what we are actually doing. All day long, we can stumble semiconsciously from one activity to another, doing each one awkwardly because

Key Words

Breathe out and stop before you start

Breathe out and stop

Stop before you start

Breathe

Stop

we're not really 'there'. No wonder we often feel anxious – we are never quite in tune with what we are doing.

If you stop before you start however, you can feel as if you are moving from one point of stillness to another all day long. Furthermore each activity will carry some of that still, present quality with it.

So breathe out and stop before you start anything new, however small. You see sports people do this all the time in preparation for a kick or a serve or a dive or a shot. I watched Maria Sharapova in a recent tennis competition. Before each serve, she would stop, turn around, look at her racket for a moment and then serve. I am quite sure she also breathed out and tried to clear the past shot from her mind as she did so. It took only a few seconds, but when she served, she was really there. To do anything efficiently, you need to be there at the start.

WHY CAN'T WE STOP?

I know it seems ridiculous, but students often tell me they can't even find the time for three sighs. Or that they find a sigh difficult to do. In fact, they are afraid to give up the habit of perpetual hurry and busyness. Their instincts are falsely telling them that even a moment's pause will undermine the fragile structure of their life. If they stop pedalling, the bike will fall over. To sigh and do nothing seems almost criminally negligent to them.

So I ask them, "Do you have time for a single sigh? Can you occasionally breathe out and stop for just five seconds?" There are actually thousands of opportunities each day. You don't even have to physically stop to do some of them. Even a mental pause will do, so

long as you really do pause. I suggest you try to breathe out and stop before you:

Make a phone call

Open a door

Walk down steps

Drive away your car

Step into the shower

Eat breakfast

Read the paper

Play a golf shot

Switch on the computer

Post a letter

Slap your child

Enter a shop

Buy the next drink

9

Soften the Body

When you recognise your breathing is tense ('holding on'), it is quite easy to relax it (to 'let go'), because your breathing is largely within your conscious control. The body is a much more complex bundle of muscles and organs and other bits, but the same principle applies: the first stage in relaxing the body is to recognise your tension and where you hold it.

When you are tense, the muscles feel tight and hard. When you relax, you'll find they feel soft and loose. By recognising that your muscles are holding on, you can usually start to loosen up within seconds. In this meditation, we particularly notice those muscles over which we have some voluntary control: eyes, face, shoulders, hands, belly. By loosening these we create a ripple effect through the deeper, involuntary muscles, which in turn helps the whole body to relax.

You could do a casual scan of the body, 'breathing through' areas of tension as you find them. That works just fine, but a more systematic way is to scan in clear stages from head to toe. There are many ways of doing this as you will see from the next chapter, but the exercise below gives you a simple seven-stage template to start with.

After two or three sighs, you breathe through the body over seven breaths, one breath to each stage. After the initial three sighs, you keep the breathing soft, or sigh gently to deepen the effect. This gives you a well-structured meditation of about a minute long. It is actually the short version of the Bodyscan meditation in the next chapter.

5. Countdown

Sigh two or three times.

Now breathe through the body over seven breaths.

Each time you breathe out, move down one region.

Silently count on each out-breath.

> *'Seven' - scalp and forehead*
>
> *'Six' - the face*
>
> *'Five' - neck and shoulders, arms and hands*
>
> *'Four' - the chest*
>
> *'Three' - the solar plexus*
>
> *'Two' -the belly*
>
> *'One' - the hips, legs and feet*

Repeat as you wish, or continue to sigh gently.

COMMENTARY

You start this meditation by sighing two or three times to loosen up the breath. Then, as you scan the body, that loose, soft feeling of the relaxed breath encourages other muscles to relax as well. Breathing is of course a muscular movement, and when any muscles relax, others start relaxing in sympathy.

It is useful to imagine you are 'breathing through' the body as you scan. If you focus on both the breath and a certain muscle group at the same time, it seems like you are 'breathing through' those muscles. Of course, the breath doesn't really go through your jaw or your hips or your ankles. It just feels that way.

By juxtaposing a relaxed sensation (the breath) with a tense one (the neck), the effect crosses over and the tense area starts to relax as well. If you do this more slowly and systematically, as described in the next chapter, you seem to gradually fill the whole body with the breath, making it feel spacious and alive.

Don't try to 'get rid of' a tension or pain by forcefully breathing through it. This would simply amplify an antagonistic attitude towards your body. Instead, you let go the out-breath and let your mind melt into the muscles as you do so. If you accept a tension just as it is, it is more likely to relax than if you try to force it. Even if that particular tension seems to remain, you'll find your body and mind relax as a whole.

COUNTING AND NAMING

You can always count the breaths to give you a clear time-structure when you meditate. The Three Sighs lasts for three breaths. The Countdown lasts for about ten breaths. As a result, this exercise encourages you to let go your usual thoughts for nearly a minute, and to focus on the sensations of the present for that time.

Counting is particularly good if you're in a distracting environment such as a supermarket queue, a red light or a lift. You need something systematic to do in those circumstances or you'll lose track as soon as you start. Counting your breaths from seven down to one is a good way to stay focused. If you don't like counting, you could say an affirmation such as 'soften' or 'let go' or 'relax' each time you breathe.

Key Words

Scan
Soften the body
Breathe through tensions

Alternatively, you could 'name' each part of the body as you focus on it, which incidentally frees you from the constraint of just seven regions. For example, you could scan by saying or thinking to yourself, 'scalp, face, neck, shoulders, arms, hands, chest, diaphragm, belly, hips, legs, feet' – breathing through each place as you do so.

Counting and naming are just devices to help you focus and you may not want to use them at all. So long as your breathing is loose, and your mind is consciously inside your skin, you're bound to relax. However, don't overestimate your ability to stay focused in the midst of distracting thoughts – it's not as easy as you think. Doing something simple and systematic, such as counting or naming, may be just what you need.

10

Scan the Body

The Countdown meditation works well for the minute or so that it takes, but it's even more satisfying to scan slowly. If you spend three or four or even ten breaths in each of those seven places, you'll feel each part loosening as you dwell on it. Your first breath simply contacts the area you're focusing on. The second breath illuminates the tensions, and by the third breath you can feel them softening. By the fourth and fifth breath…

Scanning the body slowly makes you aware of your hidden tensions, and this alleviates many of them within seconds. It is like gently combing the knots out of a tangle of long hair. You'll be amazed at how many knots you find.

In the Countdown meditation, you focus on quickly releasing the obvious tensions over ten breaths. Because scanning slowly is much more thorough, you notice not just tensions but also the whole array of subtle sensations within you: tingling, pulsing, warmth, heaviness, pleasure, flow.

This is what makes a slow bodyscan so satisfying to do. You gradually feel every part of your body reverting to a state of better health and balance. This is one of many reasons why sick people find bodyscanning so useful: it revives the memory of health. Beneath the mild discomforts or actual pain, the body can feel tranquil, radiant and vital. It feels like you're nourishing all the cells of your body just by paying attention to them.

47

6. The Bodyscan

Sigh two or three times and mentally stop.
Now scan at your own speed, spending
3 or 4 or 10 breaths in each region.

1. *Scalp and forehead*
   (Notice tingling, pulsing, pressure…)
2. *The face and lower part of the head*
   (Soften the eyes. Let the mouth and jaw go slack)
3. *Neck, throat, shoulders, arms and hands*
   (Like stroking or massaging the body with the breath)
4. *Chest and upper back*
   (Feel the lungs expand and contract)
5. *Diaphragm and solar plexus*
   (Feel the movement of the lower ribs)
6. *The belly and lower back*
   (Feel the soft organs move slightly as you breathe)
7. *Hips, legs and feet*
   (Imagine the breath dropping through your body)

Now rest in one place, focusing on your breath.
Or scan once again, up or down, as you wish.

COMMENTARY

I typically do this exercise when I'm waiting in my car, using three breaths to each area. A stationary car is a wonderful place to 'stop before you start'. You can briefly leave the world behind, and no one notices. One of my best students told me she regularly leaves home ten minutes early so she will have time to meditate in the car at the other end.

If I arrive somewhere early for an engagement, rather than stroll around or window-shop to pass the time, I consciously relax and this is how I do it: I listen to the engine die away as I switch off the ignition. I close my eyes and put my head against the headrest. I slowly scan my body to shake out the vibrations of the journey. Within two or three minutes, I can virtually put my body to sleep. Then I get out of the car refreshed and ready for the next activity.

When you scan slowly, it is common to use the breath as a timepiece. For example, you could mentally count four breaths for each of the stages above, giving you a well-structured meditation of maybe three minutes long. If you get distracted, you simply return to where you left off – the third breath in the throat, or wherever. If you want a longer meditation, you can count ten breaths in each area.

Rather than counting, you could prefer to simply feel each part of the body in detail and to move from one place to another whenever it feels right to do so. Or you could use an affirmation and say 'soften' or 'be still' or 'relax' to yourself as you scan, rather than counting.

Key Words

Soften, relax and let go
Fill the body with light
Be still
Be centred

SEVEN STAGES IS ARBITRARY

The above seven-stage division of the body derives from the yogic chakra system. When you relax deeply, you may feel a centripetal pull into what feels like the centres of those seven areas. The mind feels very comfortable and at home when it finds these inner places. When you scan, you could seek out those seven centres and rest there.

Despite the weight of tradition, it is good to realise there is nothing fixed in stone about these seven centres. They are not an absolute spiritual anatomy. The Tibetans use five centres. Different yoga traditions use more than seven. The Chinese work with a different system altogether. You're unlikely to find exactly seven chakras, unless that is what you are looking for. The sevenfold division above is only a mental template to help you structure your meditation. Change it if you wish.

Nonetheless, the feeling of these 'energy centres' is very real. If we are sensitive, we can perceive the life force in any part of the body as being either flowing or blocked or still. 'Breathing through the body' tends to soften the hard, tight areas and leads to a sense of flow and warmth, which is why we do it. Within that flow, the chakras are places that feel still and balanced and somehow spacious as well. There are scores of such places throughout the body, and they can be as small as a single acupuncture point. The mind feels drawn to such places and and it's always satisfying to let it go there.

STRETCH IT INTO A LONG MEDITATION

If you enjoy the kind of inner journey that bodyscanning involves, let me encourage you to go even slower. Although it is extremely efficient as a spot-meditation, it is even nicer if you spend ten or twenty minutes or even longer on it. This is a short meditation that naturally develops into a longer one, if you've got the opportunity.

Many of my generation of meditators (trained in the '70s) were taught to spend a whole hour doing one scan of the body from top to toe, or vice versa. You can feel the body in extraordinary detail if you try, right down to the bones and organs. The body is alive with sensation: tingling, pulsing, pressure, pain, bliss, the ebb and flow of the breath. Bodyscanning illuminates the body from within.

It is important to let your imagination tell you what to do when you scan. You could scan fast or slow, up or down, systematically or at random. I suggest you eventually customise the way you scan to suit yourself. For example, when you scan slowly, you're likely to divide the body into ever smaller parts, or to dissolve the boundaries between the parts.

Scanning downwards works with the loosening effect of the out-breath, but it can make you rather sleepy. Scanning upwards, however, by working with the energising effect of the in-breath, can keep you more alert. So you can choose to scan up or down as it suits you on any particular day.

As a further option, you could visualise. You could imagine gradually filling the body with consciousness, light or space, or a favourite colour. You could 'breathe through' blocks and pains in the body, to create a sense of bliss and flow.

Your perception of the body can change markedly when you relax. For example, when you're tense, you feel the body as being somewhat solid and hard. As you relax, however, the body feels softer and more fluid. At the edge of sleep, you may perceive the body in an almost dreamlike fashion as being numb or empty or radiant or barely there at all.

Though bodyscanning can occasionally enhance our aches and pains, it's also the royal road to bliss. It still surprises me that deep pleasure can coexist with the inevitable discomforts of having a body. Some of my students even say that severe pain or illness are no obstacles. So long as you are consciously 'in the body', and you can accept your body as it is, you are bound to relax.

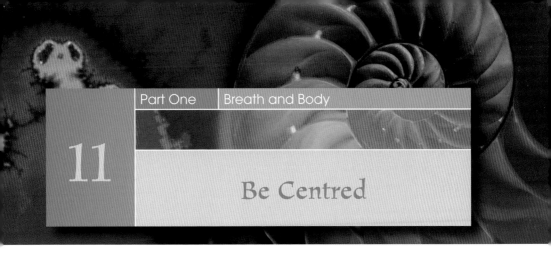

Be Centred

This meditation is as portable as the Three Sighs. You can do it while walking, standing, working or sitting. Whenever you feel hurried, just check your face and your body as a whole. They're bound to be far tighter than they need to be. While you are walking down the corridor or sitting in a waiting room, think, 'Soft eyes, soft belly'. It is like politely asking your body, 'Would you mind relaxing now?'

7. Soft eyes, soft belly

When you feel tense, think 'soften'.

Sigh, and soften the eyes.

Sigh again, and soften the belly.

Soften both eyes and belly at once.

As the eyes soften, feel your whole face go slack.

As the belly softens, feel your whole body soften.

Follow the breath to the end.

Let your mind be still.

Rest in your centre of gravity.

Continue with what you were doing, breathing gently.

COMMENTARY

By softening your eyes, you relax your mind. By softening your belly, you loosen up the breath. This exercise coaxes you towards an inner stillness. It invites your mind to settle into your centre of gravity and to feel the body relaxing around it.

Why just the eyes and the belly? These two places can each hold a huge amount of tension. They are effectively trigger points or switches. You won't relax at all if they remain tense and, alternatively, if you relax just those two places, the whole body relaxes.

Your eyes hold mental tension and the belly holds physical tension. The process of energetic thought requires a certain tension in the face, and particularly in the eyes. By relaxing the eyes, you also weaken the thinking process temporarily. And when the eyes soften, the whole face softens.

We focus on the belly for two reasons. Firstly, you can only relax the belly completely when you also let go the out-breath completely. So softening the belly automatically implies that you relax your breathing.

Secondly, in the belly is our centre of gravity, the point of balance for our whole body. The mind naturally wants to rest there when it turns inwards. The easiest way to find your centre of gravity is to follow the out-breath to the end, and to see where your mind wants to stop.

Your centre of gravity is roughly behind your navel, but don't get hung up on trying to find it exactly. Its position will be higher or lower depending on your body shape and sex, and also your mood on the day. We're actually looking for the place that *mentally* feels right: that safe, calm point of stillness and balance that is the centre of your whole being.

12

Know what it is to be Relaxed

Do you actually know what it feels like to be relaxed? Relaxation produces effects in your body and mind that are fairly easy to find if you look for them. When you're relaxed, you'll find your body commonly feels heavy, still, soft and warm, and your breathing is loose and light. If you recognise these kinds of sensations clearly they act as biofeedback, reinforcing what you are doing and taking you deeper.

Reading these little signals in detail is much more useful than simply trying to space out and feel good. Unfortunately, many people regard relaxation as a descent into unconsciousness and an excuse to tune out. As a result, they don't really notice what it feels like. It is not enough to aim for a kind of dreamy oblivion. To relax at all you need a clearer target. The paradox is that everyone relaxes – everyone goes to sleep eventually – yet hardly anyone except a meditator really knows what it feels like.

WHY WE DON'T FEEL RELAXED

There are many reasons why people relax poorly, but they usually involve being alienated from the body. A relaxed person is in touch with her body, while a stressed person lives in his thoughts. For some people, relaxation is truly an alien experience. They tell me 'I haven't felt relaxed for years.' Even in sleep their muscles are tight and they're grinding their teeth. They wake up exhausted to face yet another miserable day. It's not surprising that stress, fatigue and depression go hand in hand.

Stress makes us dissociate from our bodies. People in the trauma of an accident may feel nothing despite severe injuries. Abused children often cope by mentally splitting off, as if their bodies are not part of them. In the stress of war, young soldiers kill with a complete absence of feeling for themselves or others. When our emotions are in overdrive, we're barely conscious of the flesh and blood beneath our brains. Other matters seem far more important than our suffering bodies.

Chronically busy people are often blind to the effects of stress on their bodies. They flog their bodies along like donkeys. They may feel they're coping well because they manage to do all they have to do, but they can't understand why they also have panic attacks, insomnia, hypertension or digestive problems. There is a high price to pay for habitually ignoring the body.

Even mild stress will disconnect you from your body. Stress makes you exhausted, so when you relax at all you're inclined to space out or fall asleep. You're not there to enjoy it! Your nervous system only has an on-off switch, with no sliding scale in between. When you're awake, you're tense. When you relax at all, you fall asleep.

HOW TO READ THE PHYSICAL SIGNS

We notice tension and relaxation most clearly in the way the muscles feel. We barely feel the bones, the viscera, the brain, or the nervous system for example, although they get stressed as well. Adrenalin makes muscles contract in preparation for action: it is the coiled spring effect. Since muscles make up nearly half our body mass, the whole body feels tight and hard.

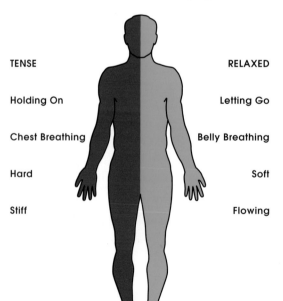

TENSE

Holding On

Chest Breathing

Hard

Stiff

RELAXED

Letting Go

Belly Breathing

Soft

Flowing

When you relax, your body typically feels heavy, still, soft and warm. These adjectives seem rather vague but they refer to precise sensations in the body. As the adrenalin charge fades, muscles loosen up and literally become softer. You can even feel that if you touch them. While you may notice this effect most clearly in the face and the shoulders, all the hundreds of muscles in the body lose tone and start to sag. The brain interprets this general sensation as the whole body feeling both heavy and soft.

Adrenalin wires up muscles and makes them agitated and jumpy, ready for action. As the charge fades, the muscles settle down and send far fewer signals back to the brain. The mind interprets this absence of sensation as the body feeling still, or even a bit numb.

Adrenalin makes the blood thick with fatty acids and cholesterol, so the heart has to pump harder to move it around a tight body. As you relax, the blood becomes thinner and your circulation improves. There is an increased blood flow to the skin, which often feels slightly tingly and warm, especially in the hands and face. As muscles become softer, we feel the increased blood flow as a warmth, or as a general sense of 'flow' throughout the body.

As we relax, our aches and pains become obvious. When muscles are tight, they restrict the flow of blood in and out of them. They become starved of oxygen and nutrients and don't expel their waste products efficiently. This oxygen starvation seems to be why the body feels sore and achy when we are stressed.

The cortisone we produce when tense is a natural painkiller which numbs sensation, but this analgesic effect fades away when we relax. Consequently, we often become more conscious of our aches and pains and fatigue. Unpleasant as these may be, they are actually good signs that you are relaxing, so you shouldn't try to fight them or make them go away. Just let them surface and resolve in their own time.

As you relax, your breathing naturally changes, as I've already explained in some detail. The breath usually becomes soft, loose, deep, delicate and light, with occasional long pauses between out-breath and in-breath.

THE OTHER SIGNS OF RELAXATION

The signs of deep relaxation are easy to recognise, but how do you know you're relaxed while walking or doing the dishes? It is largely a matter of degree. The inactive muscles will soften but not to the same degree as when you are falling asleep. Similarly, the out-breath will still be longer than the in-breath, though not quite as loose and delicate as when you're almost asleep.

You can also look at your quality of movement. When your muscles are tight, your movements are jerky and stiff, with an abrupt stop-start quality. When you're relaxed, your actions will feel smooth and unhurried. You feel more centred and 'in the body' as you move.

Furthermore all these changes are on a sliding scale between panic and stress at one end, and rest and sleep at the other. In other words, you don't instantly feel heavy and soft when you relax. You gradually slide into it, and even going part of the way with a spot-meditation is very useful.

Don't be discouraged if you can't immediately recognise all of these signs. You're probably not used to looking for them. People are also very individual in the way they feel their bodies, since body-perception is also a reflection of character and genes. Some people are born with good body awareness and others are not, although everyone can learn it.

You may personally be more conscious of the mental states – tranquility and detachment, for example – than the bodily signs. When you relax, your mind tends to be slower, more present and more 'with' whatever you're doing. It becomes still and observant, 'just watching' rather than reacting. You enjoy what you are doing and you feel calm and in control.

All that matters is that you personally know how you feel when you relax, and that you know what to aim for. Otherwise you'd never bother to do a relaxation exercise since you wouldn't notice any effect.

SUMMARY

Let me list the kinds of things you are looking for when you are relaxing:

> The body feels heavy and still
> The muscles and skin feel soft and warm
> You notice aches and fatigue more clearly
> Loose, deep breathing
> A still, clear, calm, observant mind
> A sense of balance and 'being present' and, if you're active:
> Smooth, flowing movement

13

Walk Comfortably

Walking is an excellent way to release tension, as people who go for daily walks well know. When you're tense, your body is wired-up for fight-or-flight, so the most natural release is not to sit still but to be active. Your body actually wants to run away or beat someone up or scream, but there are less antisocial ways to burn off the effects of those stress hormones. For example, you could consciously relax every single time you walked, if only across the courtyard or to the car park. You've already learnt how to relax the breathing and soften the body. This chapter explains how to do it while you walk.

Many people feel they have to be half asleep to relax at all, and the idea of meditating while you walk can seem absurd. Yet walking is as ancient a meditation posture as sitting, and often has superior results. Some people just freeze up when they sit. The rhythm of walking, on the other hand, can gently loosen the chronically tight muscles. These often need to be used a little to encourage them to let go, just as a few big sighs will help you unlock the breathing.

A stroll through the back streets, breathing easily and softening the body, could relax you much more than sitting still. The body is born to move and it enjoys it. Walking moves the juices along and keeps muscles and brain alive. The rhythm of walking has a slightly hypnotic effect that calms the mind. Walking can put you in touch with your body and with the sense world in ways that a sitting meditation is quite unable to do.

Yet walking doesn't automatically relax us. If we are anxious, we still walk anxiously, as you can see in any city street. People walk with a stiff posture, hunched shoulders and worried eyes, lost in thought. We still need to walk consciously in order to relax. Don't forget the Buddha's advice: 'When walking, just walk'.

The exercise below asks you to focus inwardly on your body when you walk, but you don't have to completely ignore your environment. Those sights, sounds, and smells are as much a part of the present moment as the tactile sensations of your body, and you can also meditate on these, as I'll explain later in the book. For the moment, however, I'd like you to focus on relaxing your breath and your body as you walk. That's the foundation for everything else.

8. Walk Comfortably

When you start walking, take three big sighs.

Sigh gently as you walk on.

Scan your body at random.

Soften the eyes, the shoulders, the belly.

Free up the shoulders and the hips.

Feel your feet swinging easily.

'Breathe through' the tensions.

Enjoy your surroundings but stay grounded.

Think: 'Breathe easily and soften the body'.

COMMENTARY

SOFTEN YOUR EYES

When we're anxious, our eyes dart around continually. Of course, your eyes have to be open while you walk, but if they're too busy you won't be able to relax. You need to settle your eyes down, while keeping your peripheral vision sharp enough to stop you bumping into strangers and tripping over kerbs. Here are three ways to do this.

First you could hook your eyes on a point in the distance – a car or tree – like casting a fishing line, and reel yourself towards it. This helps you resist the roving gaze and sideways glances. When you get too close, then cast your eyes over something else. Remember that you are not actually focusing on that object: you are just resting your eyes there. Your primary attention is still with your body.

Secondly, you could look down at the ground a few yards ahead. You can see perfectly well where you're going but not much else. Thirdly, you can let your eyes glaze over slightly. Let them rest back in their sockets and half-close the lids. Try to evoke the way the eyes feel as you come out of a sitting meditation: soft and gentle and even a little out of focus.

SCAN YOUR BODY WHILE YOU WALK

If your muscles are tense, your movements will be jerky and stiff. By paying attention and breathing gently, you should be able to walk more freely within a minute or so. When relaxed, the hips and shoulders swing easily, and your body feels more balanced. Your walking can have a beautiful, flowing rhythm to it, almost like a dance.

You start the exercise by first loosening up the breathing. Then you 'breathe through' the body and massage the muscles made tight by too much sitting and thinking. You can 'soften the body' systematically from top to bottom as in chapter 9, but I usually do a casual scan and go to the most obvious tensions in succession.

If you focus on the hips, for example, they

will soon start to move more smoothly. Then focus on the shoulders, and allow them to swing easily. Then check out other areas of habitual tension at random – the eyes, face, hands, belly, feet.

If you observe yourself carefully, you'll often find that some parts of your breathing and walking mechanisms are underused or malfunctioning, and this contributes to poor health. Habitually tight neck, shoulder and chest muscles lead to headaches, pain, insomnia and mental dullness. Flabby abdominal, hip and thigh muscles lead to a depressed posture and back pain.

This is the collateral damage of a busy life. The simplest and most thorough way to correct it is to walk consciously and breathe deeply, day after day after day. A health professional can give you good advice on how to walk, but ultimately it is up to you. If you listen to your body, you'll find that walking consciously can start to reverse the physical effects of a lifetime's stress.

WHERE AND WHEN

Walking is perhaps the most versatile of all spot-meditations. I personally do as much walking as sitting meditation each day. You can meditate any time you're on your feet – going to the shops, through the park, in a crowded street, even walking across the room. Since you can't do much else while you walk, why don't you use it as an opportunity to relax?

A walking meditation need be no more than four or five steps long. It doesn't demand you sacrifice time from some other activity. Most of us walk a kilometre or two around the house each day, and if we want, we can be fully present for each step. You'll never get that many opportunities to do sitting meditations.

If you notice the times and places when you have to walk each day, you can use them as prompts. Whenever you're in that place, a voice should pop up saying 'Do you want to meditate now?' You don't have to say 'yes' but at least you've got the chance.

We have dozens of opportunities, but the little walks that are an inescapable part of most days give us all the chance to relax regularly. These are the places where I commonly meditate:

Key Words

When walking, just walk

Soften the body

Sigh gently

Be here

From the kitchen to the computer

From one room to another

Up or down any flight of stairs

Between my front door and the car (40 seconds)

From my home to the office (5 minutes)

Walking to the post office (5 minutes)

From the carpark to the supermarket

Down the long corridor at the gym

After getting out of the car

14

Deep, Relaxed Breathing

Until now, I've suggested three distinct ways to breathe: big sighs, gentle sighs and relaxed breathing – all of which are quite natural and ordinary. The meditation below, however, is more of a breathing exercise. It asks you to use the lower parts of the lungs more than you usually do.

I know some people will immediately feel they won't be able to do it. Anxious people often feel they 'breathe badly', and think of 'deep breathing' as some impossible ideal. It almost gives them a panic attack to think about it.

In fact, deep breathing, as I explain it here, simply means to breathe as deeply as is comfortable for you. If it's not comfortable, it's not worth doing. You'll notice that whenever you relax, your abdomen loosens up, so that when you breathe in, you naturally breathe from that deeper place. In fact, 'deep, relaxed breathing' is very similar to what I call 'gentle sighing'. You put a little more effort into the in-breath, but you still let the out-breath go completely.

Deep breathing has benefits way beyond its value as a relaxation tool. It aerates the body, retards the effects of ageing and brightens your spirits. Of course, we can't focus on breathing deeply all day long, but we don't need to. Just a few minutes can make a huge difference to our well-being. I suggest my students walk and breathe deeply for at least five minutes daily. We can help keep ourselves young by expanding our lungs to their full capacity, whatever that is, for a few minutes each day as we walk.

9. Deep Breathing

When you're walking or physically active,

focus on your breathing.

Sigh a few times and let the breath relax.

Breathe consciously from low in the body.

Keep the chest inactive.

Think 'out and in', not 'up and down'.

Let go completely on the out-breath.

Wait for the new breath to come when it wants to.

Enjoy the slow, deep, smooth rhythm of this:

energetic in-breaths, but soft and loose out-breaths.

COMMENTARY

Deep breathing is relaxing because it counteracts the effect of tense, upper body, breathing. As I describe it here, a deep breath works the diaphragm and the lower ribs, but leaves the upper body more or less inactive. It is a 'deep' breath – breathing from deep in the body – rather than a 'full' breath which utilises the whole ribcage.

A sigh or a full breath goes vertically up and down in the body, while a deep breath goes horizontally out and in. While doing the exercise, it can help to think 'out and in', rather than 'up and down'.

In this exercise, you keep your attention low in the body. Push the belly and the lower ribs outwards as you breathe in, and feel them collapse inwards as you breathe out. If your shoulders rise and fall a lot as you breathe, or if your chest moves before your belly does, you'll simply reinforce the chesty habit of anxious breathing, even if you're taking in lots of air.

Even though you take a big in-breath, you still let the out-breath go completely. Remember that it is the long, loose out-breath and the little pause at the end that relaxes you. Even if you're running a marathon, you can still let the out-breath be loose. If you force it to get more air in, you'll soon start breathing from the chest and it won't help you at all.

Although deep breathing takes some effort, notice when you're putting too much effort in. If you are straining, it is probably because you start the in-breath too quickly. Don't forget to linger in that little pause at the end of the out-breath. Deep, relaxed breathing feels dark and soothing, like a deep ocean swell – quite unlike the way you breathe when you're tense.

Key Words

Deep, relaxed breathing

Out-in, not up-down

Long, loose out-breath

Don't forget your primary goal. You're trying to relax, so let the breathing be gentle and comfortable, even though the in-breath takes a certain effort. Let each breath take the shape and time that feels natural to it. You'll find that deep breathing is typically a bit arrhythmic but that doesn't make it any less relaxing. Of course, it is also good to fully aerate the lungs but that is a different goal altogether. Don't equate it with relaxing.

DEEP BREATHING SLOWS THE RATE OF AGEING

Let me scare you a little. Do you often have tight neck, shoulder and chest muscles and suffer from headaches and insomnia? These are classical signs of anxiety, chronic fatigue and, to a lesser degree, depression. Your situation may not be quite that bad yet, but I can guarantee that those symptoms will only get worse unless you do something about it.

People who suffer these disorders invariably have the jerky, chest breathing that goes with anxiety. Their neck and shoulder muscles are always tight and painful, and never relax significantly, even in sleep. A chronically anxious person couldn't even breathe deeply if she wanted to. Years of tight muscles will have compressed her lower ribcage so her lungs can't expand to anything like their full capacity.

Chronic stress and poor breathing are intimate companions. It hardly matters whether one causes the other or vice versa, because they are inseparable in their effect on the body. They both make us susceptible to illness and we age before our time.

You can monitor a person's rate of ageing by measuring his lung capacity. At seventy our lung capacity is typically half what it was at thirty, and we lose it from the bottom up. When elderly people are about to die, they breathe from only the top surface of their lungs. The lower parts generally fill up with fluid, which is why minor respiratory illnesses can be fatal for them.

Chronic anxiety accelerates our 'normal' loss of lung capacity. If you're anxious all day, that is one whole day of chest breathing in which you haven't used the lower part of your lungs. As the anxious weeks and months go by, you'll probably lose that lower capacity forever. You'll also feel older and more tired than you should.

Fortunately the cure is also obvious, though rarely developed except in the Yoga tradition. If you want to de-stress your body and improve your life expectancy, then open up your torso and breathe more freely. Keep the lower part of your breathing mechanism healthy and active. It's as simple as that but you have to keep doing it all your life. Done mindfully, the results can be better than any antidepressants or painkillers.

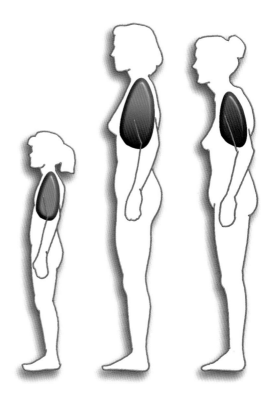

When you fill the lungs with air, you stretch the muscles of the torso the same way you expand the surface of a balloon when you blow it up. This gradually expands those muscles beyond their former limits, and makes them more supple. If you do this systematically, you can reverse the effects of years of tension, opening the lower ribcage and virtually rebuilding the structure of your body. If you remember that we lose our lung capacity from the bottom up, you can see why deep breathing, and the long, relaxed out-breath that keeps the abdomen open, are more important than simply getting lots of air in.

15

A Long Breath Meditation

If you get an appetite for short meditations, you'll find they soon tend to become longer. There is no reason why you can't scan the body or focus on the breath for thirty or forty minutes, and there are obvious advantages to this. Longer sessions relax you deeply, and return your body to that state of good functioning that is essential for long term health. A long session will also make your mind more calm, clear and insightful than a single spot-meditation can.

Although instructions remain much the same for both, long meditations require more awareness and more skill in managing obtrusive thoughts, as I'll explain in the commentary.

10. A Long Breath Meditation

Sigh two or three times.

Scan the body casually or over seven breaths.

Focus on the breath.

Let the breath be loose and uncontrolled.

Slow down and look for detail.

Feel the breath rise and fall, the body expand and contract.

Catch the end and start of each breath.

Count the breaths or say an affirmation, if yo wish.

Let your thoughts come and go.

Feel the breath gradually relax.

Feel the body soften.

Feel your mind become still.

Let your body go to sleep,

but keep your mind awake.

'Just watch' the passing thoughts

and sensations with detachment.

COMMENTARY

It is good to start any meditation with two or three sighs, and even a quick scan of the body. Then you use your mind like a zoom lens, and go to that place where you can feel the breath most clearly. It could be at the nostrils or the throat or the chest or the diaphragm or in the belly. I generally focus on my centre of gravity. Breathe in a relaxed, uncontrolled fashion, letting go the out-breath completely.

It can help to silently count the breaths to four or ten repeatedly. You would say the word 'one' on the first out-breath, 'two' on the second out-breath, and so on. If you get distracted and lose the count, you know what to do: you find the breath and start counting again. Alternatively, you could use an affirmation such as 'let go' or 'slow down' or 'be here' or 'relax' or 'be calm'.

NAME THE DISTRACTIONS

With longer meditations, you're bound to notice other thoughts, sensations and feelings coming and going through the mind. This is 'the stream of consciousness', and it never dries up no matter how peaceful you become. Whenever you meditate, there is always other mental traffic in the background.

Fortunately, you don't have to get rid of thoughts in order to relax deeply. Just let them come and go in the background. It is quite enough if you passively notice them rather than actively engage them. This is what we call 'just watching' or 'being an observer' or 'awareness'.

In fact, the core instructions for any long meditation are: 'Focus on the meditation object, while noticing other thoughts and sensations with detachment'. You can't focus so exclusively on the meditation object that you don't notice the peripheral sounds, thoughts and feelings. They are always part of the scenery and if you can accept their presence without responding to them, they won't disturb you.

Nonetheless, certain thoughts can be very demanding. You may try to focus on the breath, but you find yourself obsessing about work, or money or a person, and you just can't let go. If a particular thought is really distracting you, you can use a little technique called 'Naming the Distraction' to neutralise it.

KEY WORDS

Relax the breath

Soften the body

Still the mind

Be aware

You simply ask 'What is this?', or 'What is troubling me?', and you give yourself a few seconds to clearly identify what it is. A distraction is likely to be a thought ('work' or 'money' or 'Mary') but it could also be a sensation ('headache') or an emotion ('sadness').

By naming the distraction, you objectify it. To identify it at all, you have to interrupt the dialogue you're having with it, and see it from outside. This makes you realise you have a choice: you can continue thinking about it, or you can let it go and refocus on your meditation object. Remember that meditation is all about shifting from thinking to sensing – from your habitual thoughts to the sensations of the present. This is why it works.

Naming can break the grip of a thought immediately. Often it simply disappears. Sometimes the thought continues weakly on its own, but because you're no longer feeding it, you relax anyway. Just because you're sad or in pain or have a lot on your mind doesn't mean that you can't relax.

Naming the distractions enables you to give a little time to those matters that are troubling you, but not a lot. You can always give five seconds to a thought that really is important – you'll do so anyway – but you don't need to give it a minute. If you give a thought only five seconds rather than a minute, that is fifty-five seconds in which you are free from the stimulating effect of that thought.

THE STAGES OF A MEDITATION

Longer meditations tend to go through stages. First, the breath and the body relax, and then the mind becomes calm and clear. In effect, these are four interconnected stages, and you can use the following affirmations to identify them:

1. Relax the breath
2. Soften the body
3. Still the mind
4. Be aware

The Three Sighs meditation, for example, being very short, just works with the first stage. The Countdown and Bodyscan meditations will take you to the second stage within a minute or two. You usually reach the third stage in which the mind feels fairly still and often sleepy, within five to eight minutes. If you continue for longer, you can develop a deep stillness and that clarity of mind we call 'awareness'.

A longer meditation gives you the time to develop excellent quality in all four stages, and the key to it all is awareness. If you stay alert and consciously examine what is happening, you can fine-tune the experience so it becomes deeply satisfying. Let me describe the process, stage by stage.

Firstly, get to know the breath well. Notice how it feels when it's tense, when it is relaxing, and when it is fully relaxed. Come to know the many subtle gradations on the way, and enjoy the breath. It is much more pleasant to watch the soft, sensuous ebb and flow of the relaxing breath than to chase your usual thoughts.

Secondly, come to know the much more complex process of the whole body relaxing. Notice when muscles have started to let go and when they're completely relaxed. Bring the unconscious tensions to the surface and let them dissolve. Notice how your body feels when it relaxes fully – heavy, soft, warm, centred and still. Recognise the lovely feelings of rest and balance, and the subtle play of life inside you.

When you know your body is well relaxed, tune into your quality of mind. By focusing on the body, the mind automatically slows down and gradually becomes quite still for several seconds at a time. This calm, inward-looking state often feels pleasantly sleepy, and your mind tends to drift or daydream. Many people meditate solely for this state of semiconscious tranquility.

If you stay alert, however, you move into the fourth stage: your mind also becomes clear and aware. When your body and mind are perfectly still, you notice exactly what is happening from moment to moment, but as an outside observer. You see the contents of your mind objectively – the sensations, thoughts and feelings – and can disengage from them at will. This gives you a wonderful sense of control over your thoughts, which doesn't happen if you lapse into sleepiness.

This awareness of your thoughts and feelings often leads to understanding and insight. If, with a a calm, clear mind, you can see what is troubling you, you can gradually disarm it. Similarly, if you notice healthy ideas and feelings arising, you can develop them. The awareness alone seems to automatically dissolve the negatives and enhance the positives.

Some people prefer the sleep-like tranquility of stage three, while others prefer the clear moment-to-moment awareness of stage four, and yet both states rely on each other for real quality. You can't be deeply tranquil without a fine awareness of the process, and awareness itself is dependent on a stillness of body and mind. As a general rule, everything improves with more awareness, even tranquility.

The easiest meditations to do for longer than a few minutes are those relating to the breath and the body. This chapter, and Chapter 10, give you the guidelines you need. If you want to pursue this further, you can use the long guided meditations on my CD set called *How to Meditate*. Or refer to my other book *Do You Want To Meditate?*

Part Two

Be Sensual

16

Be Sensual

If you want to relax and 'be here', you only have to focus on the sensations of the present – sight, sound, smell, taste or touch. So far, I've asked you to focus mainly on the tactile sensations of the body. In the coming chapters, we'll use the other senses as well. But first, a few words on the value of 'being sensual'.

When you consciously taste an apple, or feel the texture of cloth or skin, or listen to a song, or smell the aroma of a flowering bush, the past and future and all their problems temporarily fade into the background. When you're actively sensing something, you marginalise the habit of incessant thought that fuels the stress response.

In fact sensing and thinking are opposing mental functions. Sensing usually relaxes you and thinking arouses you, and one tends to eclipse the other. You can't do a complex mathematical calculation and enjoy the flavour of a good soup at the same time.

Sensing and thinking use different parts of the brain, as a brain scan will demonstrate. Certain parts of the brain light up when you process visual or auditory stimuli, and different parts are used when you're thinking or talking. The active parts use more glucose and oxygen and get warmer, and the inactive parts cool down. As a result, by consciously listening or looking or tasting, you divert your energy away from those parts of the brain that think. By starving them of oxygen and glucose temporarily, your thoughts become weaker.

Thinking and sensing also produce different electrical patterns across the whole brain. Thinking results in fast, erratic 'beta' brain waves, and sensing results in the slower, more rhythmic 'alpha' brain waves. Beta occurs when you are stressed or excited. Alpha, on the other hand, being closer to your natural state of equilibrium, is more restful and uses less energy.

Sensing slows down the overactive mind. Thinking is typically fast and jumpy: you might have a hundred thoughts and shifts of focus in a minute. When we are in sensing mode however – listening to music or cuddling someone – the mind still moves but much more slowly. Sensations tend to lure us inwards and invite us to stay.

Sensing is typically more passive than thinking, and therefore burns less energy. To listen to the sounds around us, we have to sit back and wait for the sounds to come to us. Sensing is like the receptive, listening phase of a good conversation. You're not actually 'doing' anything, but it is still a skill.

Sensing sharpens the edge of the moment. It enables you to exactly notice the detail of a flavour, the subtlety of a colour, the location and quality of a sensation in the body. You only have to consider the abilities of great musicians or chefs or athletes to realise how much this skill can be developed. Just because we are all capable of listening and tasting doesn't mean to say we do it well.

It is amazing how little time we consciously spend in sensing mode – probably two or three minutes an hour on average. We live in our minds, and only check into the sense world for a second here and there so we don't bump into doors or get killed crossing the road.

If you want to be happier, try spending more time in the present. An extra five minutes each hour would be a huge improvement for most people. The intellect has its charms, but the sensate world is where you find pleasure. To enhance your feeling of well-being, I suggest you consciously taste and smell and see and hear and touch things every day. Regard it as part of your health care and stress management regime.

PRESCRIPTION

Dr. Feelgood

Go for walk
Listen to music
Good food
Red wine
Make love
Sleep well

THE DEGREES OF FOCUS

It all comes down to how deeply you focus. When we're stressed or aroused, our focus is momentary at best. A speedy mind literally speeds from one thought to another within microseconds all day long, and our ability to taste or smell or hear at all is very superficial.

The way to enhance sensing is to train yourself to focus more deeply. In practice, this means you first choose what to focus on – this breath, or this sound or this sip of wine – and then put everything else into the background. Rather like focusing a camera, you'll find your object doesn't jump into sharp focus immediately. It takes a few seconds at least for you to clear the space and to allow the object to come forward.

After you've made contact with your object, you try to sustain that contact for fifteen or twenty seconds or more before your mind drifts away. When you can do this, time seems to slow down and you notice extra detail that wasn't obvious at first glance.

Occasionally you can become so fascinated by your object that it entirely fills your mental space for a few seconds. This is when there is nothing in your mind temporarily but the breath or the music or the taste of the wine. The technical name for this state of deep focus is 'absorption' or 'oneness' or 'samadhi'.

In effect there are degrees of focus, which the Buddhist texts describe by using the metaphor of a bee approaching a flower. The very first stage is when the bee is looking for the flower but not finding it. Most of us are in this unfocused, scanning state most of the day.

You can say the bee is actually 'focused' when she sees the flower and keeps it in sight. The bee 'makes contact' when she lands on the flower

Key Words

Be sensual

Focus well

Slow down

Look for detail

Make contact

Sustain contact

Absorption

and feels it beneath her feet. She 'sustains contact' when she goes inside the flower. 'Absorption' is when she sucks the nectar, oblivious to the world outside.

These degrees of focus are quite fluid, and we typically slide up and down the scale a lot when we meditate. You can't grip on to a deep state by an act of will because good focus is naturally gentle and subtle. When your focus is strong, you virtually forget yourself and fall in love with the object. It occurs most often when you've completely lost interest in everything else. In other words, focusing is also the art of letting go.

All the exercises in this book involve focusing more deeply than you usually would. It hardly matters whether you focus on your body or an orange or an activity. It is the degree of focus, not the object, that determines how relaxed and clear-minded you become. In the chapters ahead, we'll particularly pay attention to those senses we've neglected until now – sound, sight, taste and smell.

17

Just Listen

Right now, if you put this book down and listened carefully to the sounds around you for a minute, you would relax to some degree. I can guarantee it. You may hear traffic, birds, a distant conversation or radio, then a sound from next door. Soon, you would find your face and shoulders softening and your breathing slowing down. So how does a minute's listening produce such a good result? It's not because the sounds are soothing.

Firstly, the activity of listening is much more relaxing than the activity of thinking. Listening to sounds rapidly takes you out of yourself and your mental dramas. Furthermore, random sounds are usually emotionally neutral in comparison to your habitual thoughts, and don't therefore stimulate the stress response.

Secondly, listening is almost childishly simple, and so burns little energy. You only have to listen to what is happening in this moment. And then the next moment. That's all. You are not even trying to relax, since that will happen automatically if you're in the present.

Thirdly, although the sounds are unimportant in themselves, when you're totally with a bird call or car horn, the past and future vanish. If the sounds are also beautiful or interesting, they will entice you away from your habitual thoughts.

Finally, listening to sounds will make your mind sharp and clear. You can't daydream or think about yesterday while you're trying to catch the next sound. If you listen carefully, you will find the soundscape is full of subtleties and forever changing.

11. Just Listen

Relax the body and breath.

Tune into the sounds. What is there?

Let the full range of sounds become obvious to you.

Don't reach after sounds. Let them come to you.

Enjoy the spaces between sounds.

Try to catch a new sound the moment it arises.

Listen to the sounds as if they were music.

When you drift into thought, return to the next sound.

Notice how simple this is: it's just listening.

Check your body to ensure you're actually relaxing.

COMMENTARY

Listening to sounds is a very portable meditation. You can do it anywhere and anytime – while walking, sitting, waiting, eating, dressing, going to the toilet or while trying to fall asleep. Sound is always with us – either the ambient sounds, or the sounds we make in the process of doing something.

Of course, you can also focus on the breath at any time, but if you're in a public place and you need to monitor what is happening around you, then listening to the sounds could be better. It is ideal if you're at a meeting where you don't have to do much, but you still need to act as if you're there.

People often relax in their office or workspace by 'just listening'. This helps to alert them to footsteps in the corridor

or movement at the door. If you're on public transport and your eyes are closed, the sounds will tell you when your stop has arrived.

A student told me that one morning at work had been so argumentative, she felt like quitting her job. At lunchtime, she went in despair to a park and sat under a tree. "I don't know how it happened", she said. "I listened to the sounds around me, and within a minute, I felt this deep peace come over me." A few minutes later she went back to the office and breezed through the afternoon. Nothing had been resolved. In theory it was just as dreadful as it had been in the morning, but *she* had changed.

BE AT PEACE WITH YOUR SURROUNDINGS

We may occasionally be oblivious to noise but it's impossible to block it out completely. Background noise is always with us, no matter how perfect the environment. Any time we try to relax, we'll inevitably be aware of sounds as well: the traffic, the air-conditioning, a dog barking, a car-alarm going off, a door slamming nearby, a plane overhead, or the sound of our own breathing, if nothing else.

Key Words

Just listen

Be at peace with the soundscape

Feel the space between sounds

If you feel that silence is essential for inner peace, you set yourself up for a lifetime of frustration. If you're able to meditate on sounds however, they no longer irritate you, and you can easily blend them into any other meditation you use. For example, it's not hard to focus on the breath and the sounds simultaneously. They're both right there in front of you, and it doesn't matter if your mind switches from one to the other occasionally. They both keep you in the present, and the sounds possibly more so.

THE SPACE BETWEEN SOUNDS

Listening to sounds can give you an amazing sense of space and silence. Unlike the breath or body meditations, which have an inward-looking

quality, listening to sounds takes us out of ourselves into the world around us. We may be focusing on things that are hundreds of yards away, and the mind expands to encompass them.

Random sounds give you a sense of space in other ways too. You hear one sound to the left and another far behind, and you notice the space between them. You wait in silence for the next sound to arrive. When a sound fades, you may find yourself totally alert, gazing into empty space.

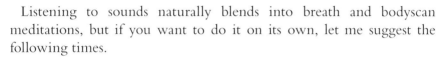

Soon you realise this background space is very stable and you can mentally rest within it. When people talk about an empty mind, this is what they mean. It's not a mental blankness, since you'll notice the next sound immediately. In fact, this space is the pure consciousness through which all our thoughts and sensations pass. Focusing on sounds can give you your first real taste of this.

Listening to sounds naturally blends into breath and bodyscan meditations, but if you want to do it on its own, let me suggest the following times.

Listen:

> Whenever you have to wait
>
> While getting dressed
>
> While in the bathroom
>
> While walking
>
> While preparing food

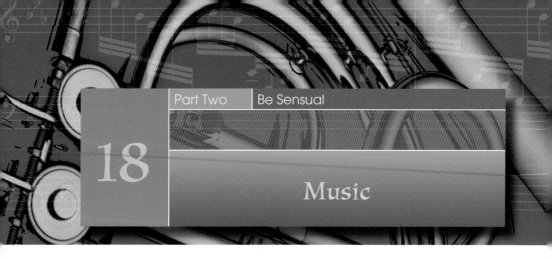

18

Music

Music is such an obvious thing to focus on. It holds our attention well and leads us along in time like an instructor's voice. If you lose focus, it's easy to find it again. Being rich in sensation and feeling, it naturally draws us away from thought.

Yet there are problems with it. Few of us are used to listening carefully to music. We commonly use it as sound wallpaper, or drift along aimlessly with it, letting our thoughts go where they will. While this may be relaxing, it won't lead to mental clarity. Only when you focus well do you discard the habit of mindless thinking.

Meditating on music should be like going to a concert. If you've paid $80 for a ticket, you don't want to space out and daydream for two hours. You want to hear what you've paid for. Fortunately, when you listen well, you enjoy the music all the more. Otherwise, you'll find yourself semiconsciously caught in thought and your contact with the music will be weak.

So while you are listening, occasionally ask yourself, 'Am I still with the music?' If you find you're drifting off into thought, then drop the thoughts and return to the music. You'll find your mind immediately becomes clearer and sharper, and the music becomes more lovely. There is a big payoff to 'being sensual'.

12. Music

Breathe out and stop.

Switch on the music.

Enjoy the colour and detail.

Let it resonate in your body.

If images or associations arise, blend them in.

Ask yourself occasionally, 'Am I still with the music?'

Notice the special live quality when you're fully there.

Feel your body relaxing around the music.

COMMENTARY

Any meditation will take us through stages of depth, and these are particularly obvious when we listen to music. Initially, the music seems somewhat distant and doesn't penetrate the cloud of our habitual thoughts. Our focus is intermittent.

Then the music breaks through and we make contact with it. We may feel it resonating in our bodies, and images, associations and feeling may arise. None of these need to be distractions. They are all part of the meditation object – i.e. the musical experience – unless you go off at a tangent with them. To check, you periodically ask yourself, 'Am I still with the music? Did I actually hear the last few notes?'

Just occasionally you become so absorbed in the music that you are aware of nothing else. You forget yourself and your problems completely, if only for a few seconds. This is when the music seems to become exceptionally beautiful. In fact it is your alert, clear state of mind that makes the music so beautiful, so enjoy it while it lasts.

WHAT KIND OF MUSIC SHOULD I USE?

People often assume they need tranquil relaxation music to meditate to, but this misses the point. It is the focusing, not the music, that calms the mind. Almost any music will do if it holds your attention. A man told me that he meditates to the frantic jazz of John Coltrane. I also find that fast complex music naturally draws me in and keeps me well focused. The kind of music you use is your choice. It could be fast or slow, tranquil or passionate, classical or modern. Any of it will work.

There are just two exceptions to this. Vocal music can get you thinking about what the singer is saying, and some New Age music is deliberately fluffy and insubstantial in order to make the mind space out. You need something clear enough to focus on, so you know when you've wandered away or not.

AMBIENT MUSIC

You can also use music to set a mood without actually focusing on it. In other words, you focus on the breath or scan the body but with soft music in the background. Obviously, you will notice the music from time to time in the same way that you notice random sounds, but it's not your main focus. When you use ambient music, be quite clear about what you are doing. Are you meditating 'with' music in the background or 'on' the music as your main focus?

Ambient music tends to act as a safety net. When your mind wanders, it tends to fall into the music rather than into your usual thoughts. The sensory qualities of music also tend to augment the sensory flavour of your meditation.

Unlike music you deliberately meditate to, ambient music needs to be quite bland. CDs of nature sounds or relaxation music are quite suitable. Anything exciting or even musically interesting can easily distract you from your primary meditation object.

Finally, the music needs to be played very quietly – about half the normal volume. When we meditate, our hearing becomes very acute. Ambient music should be so quiet that it doesn't dominate consciousness. It should be like the random sounds – something that you notice in passing and often don't notice at all.

19

Just Look

People often tell me 'I can't meditate with my eyes open'. They feel it's impossible to relax unless they escape from the world and fall into a torpor. In fact, they only need to escape from their thoughts into the slower and more sensual world of the present.

If you can relax with your eyes open, you can meditate anywhere without being noticed. You can relax in a bank queue or a meeting or a waiting room, or while walking or at the gym or doing housework. If you have to close your eyes to relax, you can't easily integrate it into your day. It remains something you can only do in private, like getting dressed or going to the toilet.

We all focus instinctively on visual objects. We look at lovely things that catch our attention during the day – a tree in full bloom, a healthy young body, a duck waddling by the lake. We stare absentmindedly at something when we get tired or bored. I suspect we've all been mesmerised at some time by the embers of a fire or flowing water. There is nothing unusual about looking at lovely objects, but it's much more satisfying to do it consciously.

You can do this meditation for just a few seconds, as I commonly do, many times a day. Or you can focus on visuals for the whole hour of a long walk. For the exercise below, however, let's assume that you want to relax while you're waiting somewhere for a few minutes.

13. Just Look

Relax your breath and your body.

Soften your eyes.

Let them blink as much as they want to.

Now focus on anything in front of you:

a leaf, a shadow, a shoe, the pattern on the carpet.

'Name' it, if you want.

Use your mind like a zoom lens.

Gently examine the detail of colour, shape and texture.

If you want, let your imagination play with the object.

Keep your eyes and your breathing soft throughout.

Feel your body relaxing.

COMMENTARY

When you start, you may be tempted to go straight to the visual object, but I suggest you still spend a few seconds relaxing your posture and breathing first. Throughout the exercise, it helps to retain a background awareness of your body, to make sure you're actually relaxing.

I usually teach this meditation by putting several objects on a low table – flowers, a candle, some fruit, a piece of driftwood, a silk scarf. Some students are interested in none of these, and focus instead on a spot on the carpet or someone's shoe. Literally anything will do.

Once you've chosen your object, let your eyes soften. When you are tense, your eyes move rapidly in their sockets, which is partly why they feel so tired at the end of a busy day. Once your eyes settle on one thing, however, they can soften almost to the point of being out of focus. And when your eyes soften, your whole face is likely to soften in sympathy.

Now let your eyes go for a lazy stroll over the object and gently observe colour and shape and texture. Look for the subtle details that you didn't notice at first glance. Let your mind absorb the features of the object like a photographic film, as if you were imprinting it in memory.

Don't blankly stare at the object in the hope that you'll go into a hypnotic trace. You focus best if your mind can get interested in the object. Remember you're doing something very ordinary. You're 'just looking' (though more carefully than usual), just as listening to sounds is 'just listening'.

FURTHER OPTIONS

These instructions come with optional extras. You could silently 'name' the object repeatedly as you breathe out. This connects the breath and the object, and gives you more to hold on to. This is particularly good if you are in a place with many distractions, such as a supermarket queue or a lift.

So if you are looking at someone's shirt in a queue, you could say 'shirt', each time you breathe out. Alternatively, if the colour is more

interesting than the shirt itself, you could say 'red'. You could even do both, saying the word 'red' on the in-breath and 'shirt' on the out-breath.

Alternatively, you could let your imagination play with the object, so long as you don't get too busy with it. Associations and images arise naturally whenever we look at something for longer than usual. This is just how the mind works. It goes through the memory bank and says 'this reminds me of that'.

You may look at a flower and remember that your grandmother had similar flowers in her garden. You look at a mango and remember the taste and texture of the last mango you ate. You could look at a small rock and imagine climbing it, as if it were a mountain. Or you see a face or an elephant in a design on the carpet. Enjoy these associations when they arise, but don't actively pursue them.

After three or four minutes, you may find you've relaxed so deeply that it is a strain to keep the eyes open. If circumstances permit, you can now close your eyes and focus on the memory of the object.

Very few people are able to imagine an object vividly, as if it was projected on a screen in front of them, but we can all remember something about it. Just to say the words, 'red rose' as you breathe would be quite enough to keep you focused. You may not be able to imagine that particular rose, but you know what roses look like – you've seen them thousands of times before. So you evoke or even construct a rose from the memory bank. Just a single petal would do. All you need is something to anchor your mind on.

BORING MEETINGS

Usually while we wait, we have to be semi-alert. It's bad form to put your head on the table and go to sleep in a meeting or lecture or waiting room, so you settle your eyes down on something and let them soften. You focus on the grain of the boardroom table, or the pattern on a chair or a dress, or the angles of the furniture.

Don't stare at your object blankly, but gently explore it, as if it were fascinating and important. Usually the object is neither, but the state of mind that you're entering is important. If you can relax frequently during the day, you're likely to be healthier and more productive than if you run on high anxiety.

Key Words

Just look

'Name' the object

Let your imagination play

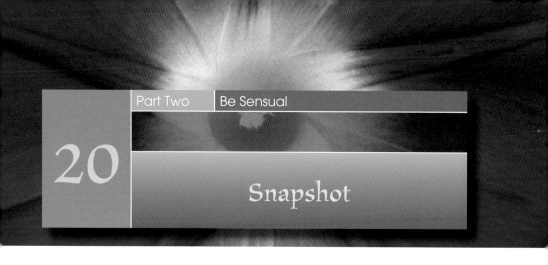

20

Snapshot

Ilove to meditate for short bursts on visual objects, usually while walking. I call this 'taking a snapshot'. I aim for a few seconds of total absorption in a leaf, a bird's feather, the bark on a tree, or a cat on a brick wall. The 'exposure' may only be five seconds, but it stops the other thoughts dead. In those few moments, I've lost myself. I'm just leaf. I'm just cat.

I imprint the image in my mind and, as I walk on, I play over the memory for the next half minute or so. It is extraordinary how much detail I can catch in a single glance. When I do this, I also find I can bring the image back to mind later in the day. For example, I can still recall the bouncy white chihuahua I saw as I walked to the supermarket a few days ago. If you take snapshots, it is easy to recall them later and relive the loveliest moments of your day. In fact, I can still remember snapshots from years ago.

This meditation is extremely short – just five to ten seconds long. You go for maximum focus in a flash, like taking a photograph, and you don't have to confine yourself to visual objects. Can you also take 'snapshots' of sounds, smells, flavours and tactile sensations? Can you replay the taste of a nectarine, the texture of your cat's fur, the sound of a flock of birds flying overhead, or the feel of the cool morning air on your face? They're all so much sweeter than your habitual thoughts.

It's good to do this systematically. Why don't you try to imprint ten beautiful sensations in your mind tomorrow? If you can enjoy the sensuality of little things, they break up the greyness and gloom of a stressful day.

14. Snapshot

Whenever you see something lovely, take a snapshot:

give it total attention for 5-10 seconds.

As you walk on, examine it in your memory.

It doesn't matter if you don't get the detail right.

So long as you're focused on something, you'll relax.

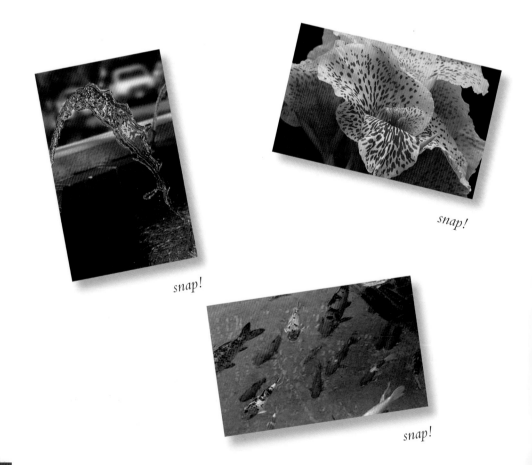

snap!

snap!

snap!

I **think we love eating so much, even to the detriment of our health, because it's often the most sensual activity of our day.** Food, like sex or pain, can temporarily obliterate the past and future. Because sensing eclipses thinking, you can always distract yourself from thought by focusing on something sensual, and food will do very nicely for this purpose.

Eating is a kind of ritualised savagery: it involves capture, biting, tearing apart, chewing to pieces and swallowing as an act of total possession. I think that eating unconsciously reassures us that we have survived another day at the top of the food chain. We can go to sleep with a full belly. The chicken, the tomatoes, the grains of rice did not survive, but we did!

If you're over thirty, and living in the West, you're probably fighting or losing the war against fat. The majority of us are heavier than is healthy, and we face food with thoughts such as, "Should I? Shouldn't I?" or 'How much should I?" Meditation can give you an unexpected edge in this war. We commonly overeat because:

1. We're anxious or
2. We're tired, or
3. Because we consume on automatic pilot.

Meditation, however, reduces anxiety and makes us less likely to reach out for the chocolate. It also makes us less tired, so we are less likely to eat for that reason. If we also pay attention to eating, we undermine the habit of shovelling food in with our minds elsewhere.

I've often noticed that meditators tend to be, if not slim, at least less plump than the average. They rarely overeat. Years ago, when I'd finished a term of teaching, I used to book out a friend's vegetarian restaurant, and take maybe sixty or eighty people there for a meal. It operated as a smorgasbord, and my friend said he would always prepare less food than usual when he knew we were coming. His usual customers would tend to gobble down their food without really tasting it, and then go back for more. My students however, tended to eat more slowly and enjoy the food in front of them. As a result, they ate less.

By eating consciously, you'll actually hear your body saying, "No, not that again!" or "Yes, I love it, but no more". Or "Don't try to pretend that you need this." This partly explains why meditators tend to be healthier and live longer than non-meditators: they're more inclined to eat the right quantities of the right food.

Of course, I can't guarantee that eating consciously will help you lose weight. You may find you love it all the more! Good cooks and gourmets are very tuned in to the sensuality of food, and it is one of the great luxuries of the 21st century that we have so much to choose from. Nonetheless, consciously eating is the way to go, and the three exercises below all point you in that direction.

Buddha's Weight Loss Pills

15. Stop before you start

Stop before you start.

Sigh two or three times. Or just once.

Start consciously.

Lift the food to your mouth.

Feel the moment of contact.

Register the taste and start to chew.

It is amazing how much food you can eat without being aware of what you are doing. It is so easy to slip something – nothing at all, really — into your mouth en route from the kitchen to the TV room without even registering it. Overeaters commonly silence their inner critic by zoning out as they munch through a packet of biscuits. You can counteract this tendency by at least being conscious of the moment you start to eat.

16. Pause between mouthfuls

After swallowing, pause.

Let the mouth empty completely.

Breathe in and out and pause again.

Then reach for the next mouthful consciously.

If we're anxious, we tend to stuff food in rapidly, like an animal that is afraid it will be robbed of its kill by a larger predator. As a result, the mouth doesn't empty before the new load comes in. In this meditation, you simply notice the end of one mouthful before you start the next.

17. Small, Slow Bites

Glance at the food before you reach for it.

Take a slightly smaller portion.

Take a slightly smaller bite.

Eat it slightly slower than usual.

When we're anxious, we tend to take big bites of food and the mouth has to work hard to break it down. Typically we swallow before the food is adequately masticated, and we send lumps down for the stomach to sort out. This is not a very relaxing way to eat.

In order to take a smaller bite, you have to notice what you are doing. You'll find there is a certain sized portion that feels right in your mouth. There will be enough space to savour the food and turn it over properly. There won't be the congestion and the pressure to swallow it too soon.

If you take small bites, eat slowly and pause between mouthfuls, you'll find your stomach is more settled as you eat. The stomach requires a certain amount of time to comfortably assimilate a consignment of food from above, so give it that time. If you feel bloated at the end of a meal, it's often because you've gulped your food. If you listen to your stomach, it will tell you when you're eating too fast.

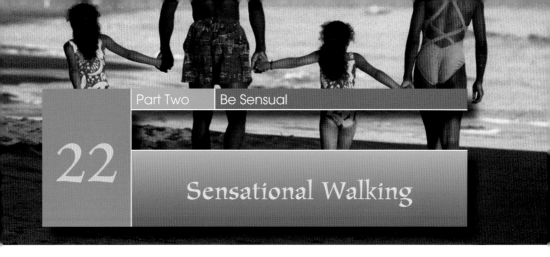

22

Sensational Walking

In an earlier chapter, I explained how to focus inwardly on the breath and your body as you walk. In this chapter, I explain how to focus outwardly on the world around you.

I suggest you select some place where you walk regularly. A two-to-five minute walk to the shops or the carpark is perfect. Once you've meditated there for a few times, it will act as a cue to remind you. Each time you enter that space, the thought will arise: 'I'm here again. Shall I relax now?'

For example, I often rise early and work, but by eight o'clock I'm ready for a break. I go to collect the mail from the post office which involves a lovely walk through tree-lined streets and attractive little houses. It only takes five minutes, so it's a wonderful opportunity to get out of my head and come back to earth. I've come to know that little journey extremely well over the years.

When you walk, you're exposed to a huge array of sensory information. It's perfectly natural to shift your focus from one thing to another, but if you shift too rapidly, you won't relax. For quality, you need to mentally slow down and notice detail. Whatever you focus on – a sight or sound or tactile sensation – you need to hold on to it for ten or fifteen seconds at least. Otherwise, you really don't connect and your mind won't settle.

In this chapter I present four different walking meditations. They differ only in what you focus on, so for convenience, I've put the instructions for all of them together. In the commentary, I'll give more details for them individually.

18-21. Sensational Walking

When you start walking, take three big sighs.

Then sigh gently or breathe deeply as you walk.

Walk comfortably and focus outwards:

1. *Listen to sounds.*

2. *Or look at one visual object after another.*

3. *Or feel the wind move over your body.*

4. *Or just be here, focusing on any sensory data.*

Mentally slow down and explore the detail.

Stay with each object for at least ten to fifteen seconds.

Keep your breathing loose and your body soft.

MEDITATION 18: JUST LISTEN

Meditation is all about focusing on one thing at the expense of all else. In this practice, you put sounds in the foreground and other sensations in the background. You choose to highlight the sounds you hear, while giving minimal attention to the objects of other senses.

When you hear a sound, linger on it. If you skim too quickly from sound to sound, you'll soon skim back into thought. Gently examine a sound before you go to the next one. Take a snapshot of any interesting sound and replay it in your mind, if you want.

MEDITATION 19: JUST LOOK

When we walk, our eyes usually scan at random, semiconsciously taking in the scene and looking out for danger and pleasure. They typically flit around, not staying with any individual object for long.

You'll find it much more enjoyable to consciously look at individual things. Let your eyes move as they wish from tree to sky to grass to footpath, but do it slowly. Remember that deep, sustained focus is much better than shallow focus in helping your mind relax. Don't go looking for something new too quickly. Wait with one thing till something else grabs you. It's much better to look at ten or twenty things in depth than to vaguely look at everything.

MEDITATION 20: WIND

This ancient practice is very sensual. You focus on the movement of air over your body as you walk or even sit outside. Even on a still day, the air masses shift around you, touching your cheek, neck or leg in succession. It feels like the earth is breathing over you. It's quite passive, like listening to sounds. You just wait for the next lick of air on your skin.

MEDITATION 21: BE HERE

The earlier exercises invited you to primarily focus on one sense – sight, sound or touch. In this one, you combine them, and can even include the sense of smell as well. You focus on whatever sensation catches your attention in the moment, and shift your focus as you wish.

What makes this different from a stroll in the park is that you linger with each thing for at least ten seconds until something else replaces it. You sink into the detail: the smell of the earth, the sight of birds fighting, a blast of wind in your ear, the crunch of gravel underfoot. Yet it's still a discipline. The sensory world is vast but it still has boundaries. Notice when you're wandering back into your habitual thoughts, and return to the present.

Key Words

Just listen

Just look

Feel the wind

Be here

Coffee

Ioften **meditate on food or drink when I'm eating in company.** If I'm at a cafe or a dinner and I find my head is spinning with the buzz of the conversation, I deliberately withdraw into myself for a minute or two. I don't want to be any more reclusive than I am already so I discreetly take a sip of coffee or a bite of food. That's the whole meditation, but it can seem to take a long time. It goes something like this:

First, I take a deep breath or two and adjust my posture. Then I slowly reach out my hand, feel it make contact with the cup and then feel the muscles tense to raise it to my lips. I consciously smell the aroma, tilt the cup, feel the froth and the liquid coming through my lips.

I move the coffee around in my mouth, and feel my salivary glands respond and swallow. Then I deliberately put the cup down, noticing the very moment that my hand separates from the cup, while I continue to savour the vanishing tastes in my mouth. I relish the space this activity has given me, and when ready, I return to the conversation. Obviously, I can do exactly the same kind of thing with a mouthful of food.

The exercise below clearly illustrates what it means to 'do what you're doing.' I'm actually focused not on one thing but on a sequence of many small, distinct movements. As I explain more fully in Part Three, this awareness inevitably makes my actions more smooth and flowing. All this makes a single sip of coffee a very enjoyable meditation.

22. Coffee

Breathe out and stop.

Mentally prepare yourself for the coming action.

Can you do it with perfect efficiency and grace?

Reach out your hand deliberately.

Pick up the cup, and raise it to your lips.

Pause. Look. Smell.

Now tilt the cup and feel the liquid flow into your mouth.

Enjoy the pure luxury of it.

When you're ready, swallow.

Slowly return the cup to the saucer.

Feel the very moment the activity ends.

Notice how still your mind has become.

Or this...

Be Sensual:
Look
Touch
Smell
Taste…

Part Three

Do what you are doing

24

Do What You Are Doing

'Be Here Now', said the hippies in the '60s. 'When eating, just eat', said the Buddha. 'Don't worry. Be Happy', said Meyer Baba. Many gurus teach that we should eradicate all traces of the past and future from consciousness, and live completely in the moment.

Maybe hippies and monks and children can live this way, but not you or I. While shopping or driving the car, we typically think forward and back as well, processing the thoughts, feelings, memories and problems that flow through our minds. By doing routine activities on automatic pilot and *not* being in the present, our minds are free to simultaneously do other things as well. We couldn't function at all without this ability to 'multitrack'.

So why should we listen when the Buddha says 'When eating, just eat'? For many of us, the multitracking is way out of control. It is a noisy, headlong riot that achieves nothing but confusion and fatigue. Consumed by thought, we spin out and lose all contact with the sensory ground of our being. We literally don't know where we are.

We can't live permanently in the present, but we should be able to return there whenever we want to. If we focus on what we are actually doing, we can rapidly slow down from the racy speed of thought to the slower pace of the sense world. It is much more sane and healthy to 'be here' when we can, just eating breakfast or just watering the garden, than to multitrack obsessively all day long.

FOCUSING ON AN ACTIVITY CAN BE TRICKY

Until now, I've invited you to focus on the body or on individual sensations. It's quite a different matter, however, to focus on an activity. It is all very well to relax with eyes closed in a chair, but what does it mean to be fully present and relaxed while eating, doing the dishes, getting dressed, playing with your dog or doing the shopping?

An activity is a more complex thing to focus on than the breath. Firstly, it is not one thing. Most activities consist of a sequence of rapidly changing micro-actions. The theory of 'doing what you are doing' is easy to understand, but the fluidity of even simple tasks can confuse you.

You can be very relaxed while you're active, but it may feel quite different from a sitting-down-eyes-closed meditation. As the activity changes, you'll notice a large variety of sensory data: sounds, tactile sensations, visuals, even smells and tastes. All of these can keep you present, but the effect is more vivid than focusing inwardly on the breath. You can easily be distracted and you may not be sure that you are relaxing at all.

BE SYSTEMATIC

Unless you deliberately train yourself, to 'do what you're doing' is likely to remain a good idea that never quite delivers the rewards you expect. The following five chapters map out ways of developing this skill.

Firstly, you acknowledge what you are doing by 'naming' it. Naming the main activity ('shopping') orients the mind and gives you a target. Naming the micro-actions however ('picking up, putting down, waiting, choosing') is what really draws you into the moment.

Secondly, you acknowledge the moment the micro-actions stop and start. You notice the split-second when you pick up a can of fish and the split second when you drop it into the shopping basket. You complete an action consciously and start the next one consciously. It is impossible to multitrack while doing this.

Thirdly, you get right into the middle of any action. You slow down mentally, if not physically, and become engrossed in the sensory detail of each micro-action. You feel the shifting muscle tension in your arm as you reach out. You feel the texture and resistance of the door handle as you pull it.

Fourthly, you notice how you are doing an action. Are you tense or relaxed? Are your movements tight and jerky, or do they flow? With awareness, you can always make your movements more smooth and flowing. A relaxed action has a certain graceful harmony to it, even if you're just picking up the telephone.

Finally, you check your speed. Anxiety will make you hurry and fuss unnecessarily. For any activity there is a right speed for maximum economy of effort – not too slow nor too fast. If you look, you will find exactly the right pace as you put away the groceries.

The spot-meditations in these five chapters come as a package, giving you different ways of entering the same space. These exercises all interconnect, and it's up to you what you emphasise. When it 'clicks', and you can simply 'do what you are doing', there is an exquisite sense of balance and rightness to your actions.

So do you actually want to learn this? The body- and sense-based meditations in Parts One and Two will be quite satisfying enough for some people. They are simpler to do and easier to understand, since they are natural developments of what we do intuitively anyway.

In contrast, the following five chapters take you into new territory, and it can take some imagination to get comfortable there. If you get skilled at focusing on activities, however, you can be relaxed, clear-minded and fully present for two or three hours a day more than you would normally. This is how spot-meditating can make a qualitative shift in the flavour of your life. If you can get the knack, it is well worth the effort.

Key Words

Name the action
Notice stops and starts
The middle of the action
Smooth, flowing movement
The right speed

CHOOSE YOUR ACTIVITY

These skills can be applied to a vast variety of activities, but I suggest you start modestly. Choose just one daily activity, and practise it for several days in a row. Don't try to conquer the whole world at once. Carefully colonise your daily landscape, activity by activity.

Certain activities are well suited to longish spot-meditations. I recommend you choose any one of the below and try to make a routine out of it:

Getting dressed

Doing the dishes

Tidying up

Preparing food

Ironing

Having a shower

Eating

Going to the toilet

Shopping

Exercising

It is best to aim for short sessions of high quality. It is easy to be fully present for the minute or so that you go to the toilet. On the other hand, your focus can get a bit fuzzy in the twenty minutes it takes to make a meal.

Be realistic with your expectations. At first, you'll probably get distracted and lose focus on your chosen activity long before you get to the end of it. Don't be annoyed. Just refocus. It is quite hard to stay on track to the very end – even the Buddha acknowledged that – so don't make the end too far away at first.

So for a few days, try to get dressed, or have a shower, or make a cup of tea consciously. The first few times will feel quite pleasant, but after a week or so, the quality may change utterly. The change is likely to appear in momentary flashes: little epiphanies of stillness and brilliance. The water in the shower or the toothbrush hanging in space. The air on your skin like you've never felt it before. These are little doorways into a radiant present and although they rarely stay open for long, you start to realise what 'being here' really means.

While regularly practising with one activity is important, don't forget to be spontaneous. A spot-meditation can be just one mini-action long. When stretching, say 'stretch' and stretch totally. When yawning, get right into the yawn. When scratching your ear, just scratch, being as self-absorbed as a dog or cat would be. When brushing your teeth, notice all the multisensory detail. And, as always, relax your breathing and keep your body soft while you do so.

Meditation Sanctuary

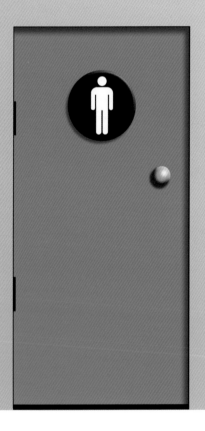 

25

Name The Action

We typically do mundane activities in a kind of mild trance. We vaguely know that we're eating or hanging out the washing but, while doing so, we could be mentally in Berlin or the year 2001. By 'naming' the activity, you acknowledge, 'this is what I'm doing and I know that I'm doing it'.

If you find yourself caught in a riot of scattered and anxious thoughts, this little technique will help you escape. When the multitracking is running wild, you 'name' what you are actually doing. You bring the action from semiconsciousness into full consciousness, which thereby gives you a chance to reconnect with the here and now.

If you're shopping, you say 'shopping'. If you're cooking, you say 'cooking'. You can say the word each time you breathe out like a chant, or simply think it once or twice. It is a way of extracting yourself from runaway thought and inviting yourself back to earth.

Naming an activity ('cooking') orients you to what you're doing and gives you a target. However naming the micro-actions within that activity ('opening, picking up, pouring, putting down') is what draws you into this very moment. It is up to you how precise you want to be. You can either *name* or simply *notice* the micro-actions. Either way, you try to mentally register exactly what you are doing at a particular moment.

23. Name the action

Breathe out and mentally stop.

'Name' the action and the micro-actions.

Continue doing what you are doing.

Slow down and notice sensory detail.

When you know you're 'here', stop naming.

Simply 'notice' the micro-actions.

Move in a smooth, unhurried fashion.

COMMENTARY

When you 'name' an activity, it is useful to say that word repeatedly for a while in time with the out-breath. This gives the naming a slightly hypnotic, chant-like quality which encourages you to focus on the action. Naming doesn't disturb the activity at all. In fact, you usually do it more smoothly and gracefully if you remind yourself what you are doing.

Alternatively, you may prefer to say the word only one or twice, to orient you at the start. Once you've clearly made that shift from thought into sensation, and you feel you're well focused, the naming can be redundant. If your mind drifts away from the activity, however, you can start naming it again.

By the way, a typical naming word, such as 'eating' or 'walking', is likely to end with an '...ing'. I find this cumbersome, so I usually just say 'eat' or 'walk' instead.

GO FOR QUALITY:
NOTICE THE MICRO-ACTIONS

As you focus more carefully, you'll soon find your activity subdividing into many individual micro–actions. This is how the moment really becomes alive. While you're 'Getting dressed' for example you may say 'open, choose, close, bend, pick up, put on, button, tie etc.' When you're 'Doing the dishes', your naming words could be 'turn on, turn off, scrub, put down, smell, scratch nose…'

Fairly rapidly, you'll find that even the micro-actions start subdividing. 'Scratching', for example, can become 'lift the hand, touch, first scratch, second scratch, nose twitch, rub, lower the hand, etc.' At this point, it is obviously far too awkward and counterproductive to name, so you stop *naming* and simply *notice* the micro-actions.

The purpose of naming is to pull you into the action. When your attention becomes this exact, it is almost impossible to multitrack at the same time. The past and future vanish utterly. Once your mind has slowed down enough to notice the sensory detail of a micro-action, and its start and finish, and how distinct it is from the other actions that frame it, you hardly need to name as well.

However, please don't use this as an excuse to be lazy about naming. Naming is one of those maddeningly precise, pointy-edged skills that can have astonishing results. Even if great athletes in training don't literally name what they are doing, their patient eye for microscopic, moment-to-moment detail is one essential skill that distinguishes them from the crowd. You have to let the naming go at a certain point, but don't let go too early.

With practice, you'll start to realise what 'doing what you are doing' really feels like. It can make an ordinary thing feel startlingly alive and beautiful, if only for a second. Just to slice the tomato, or to tie your shoelaces consciously, can feel utterly different from

ACTIONS:

walk
eat
drink
shop
exercise
cook
clean up
dishes
iron
shower
get dressed
drive

MICRO-ACTIONS:

open
close
pick up
put down
turn on
turn off
bend down
stand up
wash
dry
scrub
itch
clean

semiconsciously doing the same thing. You'll find your usual hurry and worry have temporarily vanished. You may also feel a gentle satisfaction with what you are doing – just tying up your shoes, breathing gently – what perfection!

brush

sneeze

yawn

scratch

stare

touch

let go

choose

brush teeth

dry hair

flush toilet

walk in

walk out

step up

step down

hang up

throw out

carry

give

take

26

Stops And Starts

Naming an activity such as 'shopping' will divert you from thought, but tuning into the micro-actions is what really brings you back to earth. This exercise takes you a stage further: it asks you to notice the exact moment that one micro-action stops and the next one starts.

Can you consciously complete one action, pause for a nanosecond, and consciously start the next? Paradoxically, the pause takes no time at all, but without it you're unlikely to notice the exact start of the next action. You'll already be into the action before you realise it.

So finish tying up your shoes, pause, then stand up.

Put down the phone, pause, then pick up your pen.

Pick up your toothbrush, pause, open your mouth.

Turn on the ignition, pause, then shift into gear.

Flush the toilet, pause, then turn to the sink.

For myself, I particularly like to notice the exact moment I touch something – a door handle, a piece of clothing, a dish, a pen – and the exact moment I let it go. I also do this exercise by noticing the exact moment I breathe in and the moment I breathe out. When walking, I notice the moment I pick up my foot and the moment I put it down.

The endings can be quite elusive. We can do most things semiconsciously, but we have to be fully conscious to catch the exact instant an action stops. It really is a nanosecond – the moment when your hand releases the cup, when you swallow the last fragment of food, when you close the car door. Some people never notice these endings: the future is incessantly, urgently calling them on...

24. Stops and starts

Breathe out and stop.

Slow down and notice the micro-actions.

Notice the exact finish of an action.

Pause for a nanosecond.

Consciously start the next action.

Notice when that one finishes.

Pause for a nanosecond.

Consciously start the next action, and so on.

COMMENTARY

The Three Sighs takes about twenty seconds to bring you to a halt, resting in that pause at the end of the breath. The Stop Before You Start exercise takes only one sigh and five seconds, so it's even easier to integrate into your day.

In this meditation, you pause for just a nanosecond. It feels like a pause, but it is more like a moment of clear recognition that may take literally no time at all. It doesn't obstruct what you are doing. You could easily do it a few hundred times in a day. It doesn't slow the action significantly: it simply slows the headlong race of your mind. All this exercise asks is that you acknowledge the exact end of an action and the start of the next.

Noticing stops and starts takes a little mental precision and sensitivity, but you don't need to be tight about it. You can still do it in a relaxed manner with your breathing soft and loose. The results can be exquisite: clear, crisp sensations and a moments of stillness and space. Make sure you enjoy it. Noticing stops and starts can be the most perfect way to escape the past and future and the habit of multitracking.

This modest little practice can have remarkable effects. Your mind can become very still, clear and observant, and this mental quality can continue after the meditation is over. Furthermore, if your mind becomes racy again, just a few seconds noticing stops and starts will realign you.

You'll also find that to be fully conscious of an action soon improves the quality of your movement, as I explain in the next three chapters. You'll feel more in touch with the action (Chapter 27). Your movements will soon become smoother and more co-ordinated (Chapter 28) and you will move at the right speed (Chapter 29).

CONSCIOUSLY START

If we're always restlessly hurrying, we're forever stumbling into the future. We typically find ourselves in the middle of an action before we realise what we are doing. Our starts are usually wobbly, and this contributes to our usual anxiety. If you're not really there at the start, how can you be sure you're doing that thing right?

If you notice when a micro-action stops, however, you also become able to consciously start the next one. Noticing the stops and starts means you effectively acknowledge 'I've stopped that and now I am going to start doing this.' You become alert enough to catch that brief moment of intention that precedes any action, however modest.

By pausing for a nanosecond and consciously starting a new action, you're bound to do it more efficiently. This takes no effort on your part: the awareness alone cleans up the act. You'll find that you do the action in a relaxed and balanced fashion. Your movements won't be jerky and abrupt. They'll have a certain flow to them, whether you're picking up the telephone, or putting away your clothes, or taking the groceries out of the car.

While doing so, you'll also find your chronic habit of worry and hurry has evaporated. That nanosecond between actions can be exquisitely still and peaceful, and that tranquil mood can infuse the actions that follow. If you notice stops and starts for long enough – just a minute will do – your shoulders will drop, your breathing and body will soften, and the mind will shed its obsessions. The walk from the supermarket to your car can seem like an eternity of freedom and space.

Key Word

Stop, pause, sta

27

The Middle Of The Action

Occasionally you can become so absorbed in an activity that the rest of the world vanishes. Nothing else distracts you and the past and future are completely off the map. We can get lost in music, gardening, video games, exercise, nature, rage, eating or drinking, poker machines, lovemaking, sport or anything that enthrals us for good or bad. Obviously, we have to be careful what we get absorbed in.

These states are typically brief but intoxicating, partly because they are such a perfect escape from our usual concerns. The great meditation traditions all aim for such states of absorption, which are variously described as ecstasy, oneness or 'samadhi'. The exercises in this book, which are derived from those traditions, lead stage by stage towards this.

Part One gave you the foundation, by showing you how to relax the breath and the body. The next stage is to Name the Actions and the micro-actions to orient you to the moment. Then you consciously Stop and Start in order to be fully present for at least a nanosecond at a time.

This next exercise coaxes you further into the action. You aim for an uninterrupted continuity of focus, so you feel the activity from inside. When you do so, the sensory detail becomes exceptionally clear. You feel that the arrow of time has stopped, and this moment is all there is. Paradoxically, your mind feels both tranquil and alive. You feel almost in love with what you are doing. You'll soon realise this feeling of being completely at one with an action is quite different from 'more or less' being present.

25. The middle of the action

Breathe out and stop.

Slow down and notice detail.

Notice the stops and starts of the micro-actions.

Mentally get inside the activity.

Feel still and focused and in the

moving centre of each small action.

Feel the subtle movements within your body.

Notice tactile and visual sensations.

Notice when you're fully 'there',

or when you're just in the general vicinity.

COMMENTARY

The Buddha suggested we notice the start, middle and end of literally every perception, and to start by practising with the breath. In general, you won't notice the 'middle' unless you first notice the starts and stops that frame it. The start and finish of the in-breath and out-breath are relatively easy to notice, since those are precise moments in time, but the middle of the in-breath and the middle of the out-breath are not, and this is what makes them so interesting.

By pointing to the middle, the Buddha is asking you to notice the whole shifting sequence of sensations that occurs over a single breath. The whole muscular process is subtle, fluid and complex. You can't possibly 'name' what is happening, but you can allow it to fill your consciousness. Moment to moment, you can be 'inside' the changing breath.

This is good focus. When eating an apple, you feel the contact of your teeth on the skin, the 'snap' of sound as you bite, the rush of juice and saliva. When you hang out wet washing, you feel the muscle resistance in your arm change as you raise it from the basket to the line. When you sneeze, you feel the whole shivery sequence from the tingle to the

release and after. When you walk up steps, you feel the repeated shift from balance to tension and back to balance again.

States of absorption illustrate a basic principle in meditation. To calm the mind, you slow down and notice detail, and in fact any kind of sensory detail will do. You don't even have to do the action any slower: you just slow the speed of your mind. If an activity fills your mental space, your habitual thoughts can't get a foothold and your mind becomes calm and clear.

When your mind is at one with your body, you inevitably move more gracefully. Firstly, the quality of your movements becomes smooth and flowing. Secondly, the speed will be right. If 'to get inside the action' is not an easy concept for you to grasp, you could alternatively focus on those two factors – the quality and speed of your movements – and you'll get much the same result. I'll talk about these in the next two chapters.

28

Smooth, Flowing Movement

We can do any action in a tense or relaxed fashion. If you cut a tomato when you're tense, your movements will be hurried and inefficient. If you cross the room worrying about money or your daughter, you'll use twice the energy you need for that little journey. It can take a lot of effort and kilojoules to keep your face and shoulders and belly screwed up for those few steps.

If you're relaxed however, and 'just walking', your movements will be smooth and flowing. You'll burn just the right amount of energy for the task. The more you consciously get 'inside the action', the more fluid and graceful your movements become.

The last spot-meditation, The Middle of the Action, attunes you exactly to what you are doing. This meditation asks you to notice how you are doing it. Unlike the Stop and Start exercise which creates tiny punctuation marks in an activity to slow your mind down, this exercise invites you to make your movements smooth and connected. Once your mind is fully present, you can focus on your quality of movement without getting speedy again.

26. Smooth, Flowing Movement

Do what you are doing.

Notice the stops and starts of the micro-actions.

Get inside the action.

Are you moving in a tense or relaxed fashion?

Make your movements smooth and graceful.

Think 'smooth, unhurried movement'.

Move at just the right speed.

Breathe easily and keep your body soft.

29

The Right Speed

Let me suggest that for every action, there is a right speed – not too fast nor too slow – for maximum ease and efficiency. When you're stressed, you will almost certainly be moving too fast or alternatively dragging your feet with exhaustion. This next spot-meditation gives you yet another way to relax. You simply ask, 'Is this the right speed?' Or, 'Am I moving in a smooth and unhurried fashion?'

If you're not, it's perfectly obvious what to do. Of course it's easy to slow down briefly, but unless you stay focused, you'll soon bounce back to your original speed. To move at the right speed implies many of the things we've dealt with in previous chapters. You consciously focus on what you're doing; you 'get inside the action', and you make your movements smooth and flowing.

So can you do the following at the right speed?

Open a cupboard door

Pick up a towel

Address a letter

Walk through a doorway

Read the paper

Chew a mouthful of food

Close the curtains

Drive around a corner

And if you are doing several things in succession, can you move between them in a smooth, unhurried fashion?

27. The Right Speed

Breathe out and stop.

Notice what you are doing.

Gradually 'get into the action'.

Notice your speed. Is it too fast?

Are your movements jerky and abrupt?

Think 'smooth, unhurried action'.

Breathe gently or sigh.

Move at the right speed for that action.

COMMENTARY

DON'T HURRY

Stress literally speeds us up. Adrenalin stimulates your body to make more energy available for fight or flight. With those extra kilojoules flowing through your bloodstream, you move faster and feel you have to hurry, whether you need to or not. Stress is like pressing the accelerator pedal – it converts into speed. Worry translates into hurry.

Unfortunately, adrenalin, speed, effort, worry and desire rarely give you the results you hope for. Burning energy fast is wasteful and damaging in the long run. When stress fires you up, like taking a shot of coffee, the mind and body often function very well for a few minutes. Thereafter, it's all downhill.

Worry gives you minutes of peak performance followed by hours of agitation. Similarly, if you're speedy for years, your career may leap ahead at first but in time the speed will disable you. Many successful people are on-the-go perfectionists who increasingly suffer from chronic anxiety and ill-health as they get older. In all kinds of subtle and obvious ways, speed is a killer.

Hurrying makes you feel you're doing things efficiently but your instincts are deceiving you. Does tidying up the house in a jerky, scattered, intense manner really get things done any quicker? It may feel that way but really, how much quicker?

Key Words

Slow down

The right speed

Don't hurry

Does an hour of hurry even give you an extra minute free at the end? And at what price?

Hurry leads to exhaustion. Worry leads to anxiety and misery. Constant hurry will make you feel constantly stressed, exhausted and miserable. Even worse, you could have tidied the house, and lived your life, in a relaxed, well-paced manner and got everything done anyway.

The habit of hurry may involve a literal addiction to adrenalin. This even includes withdrawal symptoms when you relax. Stressed people often feel quite bad, both physically and mentally, when they slow down. Hurry can mask your mental agitation and stress-related pains, none of which are pleasant to recognise. It can be quite alarming to realise that you are running on empty and that you feel rotten. You may also feel that hurry is what holds your life together and that slowing down, or occasionally stopping, would lead to catastrophe. All this can make the habit of hurrying very difficult to break.

It is quite possible to cure your addiction to hurry and worry, but it takes training, some of which is cognitive. Don't believe that voice that says you have to hurry all day long. It's lying, as any rational analysis will show you. However, if you want to break the habit, you can't just argue with yourself about the value of slowing down. You also need to change your body's physical responses.

The above exercise recalibrates your habitual levels of arousal. If you're racy, then slow down just 10%, many times a day. Sighing helps a lot. If you can move at the right speed for any activity, you can gradually persuade your body to cut back on its daily intake of adrenalin. The payoff can be wonderful, both on the spot and in the long term, but if you want to reverse the effects of years of stress, you do need to keep at it.

Computer crash? Kids making a mess? Far too much to do today? You can still cruise through, just doing one thing at a time. At a certain point, you will find that events that used to propel you into manic behaviour no longer do so. That's a sign of accomplishment. Time for a celebratory cup of coffee!

Not too fast, not too slow, just right…

30

Using Words

If you're stressed and your mind is overrun by pointless chatter, you may be inclined to think of meditation as the opposite state: a blank space completely free of words. However, you don't have to regard words as the enemy. They can be invaluable when you relax. Words and thoughts can be terrible masters but they make wonderful servants. After all, you are using the words in this book to learn this skill. Furthermore, you can use key words while you meditate to clarify the experience.

Words are just aids, but they can be very useful ones. If you can articulate what you are doing, you are likely to do it so much better. I find that people who are reluctant to use words when they meditate often get lost in a dreamlike fog, which is not that useful.

In Chapter One, I explained how to use a key word or phrase as either a trigger or as a chant or as a guiding concept. You could either say the word once to initiate the practice, or chant it silently in time with the breath, or mentally hold the idea throughout to remind you what you are doing. If you reread those instructions, having come this far in the book, they'll make more sense to you now.

You can also use words in other ways. At any moment, you can 'name' what is happening in consciousness, be it a thought, feeling or sensation. You can also 'name a distraction' to disarm it. You can name the stages of a meditation. And you could use a word as a subject for contemplation. Let me now explain these in more detail.

NAME WHAT IS HAPPENING

While counting the breaths, for example, you may notice that you are starting to feel heavy or soft. If you say 'heavy' or 'soft' for a few seconds, you bring those sensations into full consciousness. This acts as biofeedback and amplifies their good effect. Conversely, if you consciously acknowledge a noise or a pain, this tends to minimise your reaction to it.

NAME THE DISTRACTIONS

If you are getting distracted and can't focus on what you are doing, then it helps to 'name the distraction'. You simply ask 'What is this?', or 'What is troubling me?', and you give yourself a few seconds to clearly identify what it is. A distraction is likely to be either a sensation or a thought or an emotion. For example, it could be a headache or an obsessive thought about work or you may just feel sad or irritable.

By 'naming the distraction' ('pain' or 'work' or 'anger') you objectify it, and this gives you a choice. You can continue to wrestle with it, or you can let it go and refocus on your meditation object. Naming doesn't necessarily get rid of a thought, but it places it in the periphery of your mind. You don't have to give it full attention. Just because you're sad or in pain or have a lot to think about doesn't mean that you can't relax as well. (See Chapter 15 for more about 'naming the distractions'.)

NAME THE STAGES

You can also use words to name the stages of a meditation, rather like mentally going through the instructions. When you focus on breathing, then say 'breathe'. As you move on to softening the body, say 'soften'. As the mind settles, say 'be still', and so on. The following chapters on yoga and gym work give you examples of six or eight words to use as trigger points within a single exercise.

CONTEMPLATE AN IDEA

Finally you can use words to understand a concept or experience more deeply. What does it really mean to be calm, or mentally clear, or centred? What does 'peace' or 'love' or 'fear' really mean? What is the gut-feeling around a particular image or experience?

To contemplate an idea means that you first 'name' it. You hold that word gently in your mind, and wait for associations and insights to gradually appear around it. Remember to stay grounded in your body and don't chase after the thoughts. It is much better to feel the emotion and bodily sensations around an idea than to spin out verbal commentaries on it. Also remember that the calm, clear state of mind that leads to insight is much more valuable than any individual thought. Don't forget to feed the goose that lays those golden eggs.

To summarise, you can use a word or phrase:

1. As a trigger
2. As a chant
3. As a guiding principle
4. To identify what is happening
5. To name distractions
6. To initiate the stages of a meditation
7. As a subject for contemplation

Part Four

Exercise

31

Exercising To Relax

Ihave an elderly friend who was a Buddhist monk for many years. When his doctor suggested he attend a gym to build his muscle tone, he found he would slip into a meditative trance while on certain machines. Eyes closed, he would cycle into Heaven or sit motionless at the end of a set, much to the concern of his instructors. "Are you all right?" they would ask, until they understood his peculiarities.

We don't usually think of a gym as a place of inner peace. Amid the heaving bodies and clunking machines, there are often TVs and radios playing, yet many people (though not all!) find it a wonderful place to relax. Similarly, when people run or swim or walk for their health, they often feel refreshed in body and mind afterwards.

So why can exercise have such a wonderful result? Firstly, any repetitive exercise can have a soothing, hypnotic effect rather like chanting a mantra. It's much more relaxing to repeat one action again and again than to think about a dozen things simultaneously.

Secondly, exercise gets you out of your head. Even if you are working out mechanically, you'll still notice your body more than while operating a computer. It is even better if you actively focus on what you are doing, and some forms of exercise – yoga, tai chi or gym work, for example – demand this if you want quality.

Thirdly, exercise is relaxing because muscles need to be worked fully to relax fully. Underused muscles get stiff and painful, which is why a sedentary life, which might seem to be physically undemanding, can actually lead to chronic tension and even disability in time.

BE RELAXED WHILE YOU EXERCISE

I always admire people who manage to exercise regularly, and I'm pleased with myself when I can do it. Finding the time and motivation is not easy, and it's not surprising that only 20% of the population manage it. Exercise done well can be glorious, so it saddens me to see dedicated people exercising in ways that are neither relaxing nor efficient.

At the gym, the mothers hurry through their routine: they feel they're selfishly stealing time from other responsibilities. The fanatics strive for the impossible. Others are engaged in a remorseless battle with the Grim Reaper or their weight. Some dutifully exercise as a miserable chore – doctor's orders – with their minds elsewhere. Most hold their breath unnecessarily or tense up muscles they don't need.

The common illusion is that exercise is so much better if it's 'hard', and that a good workout is when you feel stuffed afterwards. The reality is that if you're relaxed – just doing what you are doing – you'll be more efficient than if you strain.

Great athletes know about being economical with their energy. If you're relaxed and pacing yourself well, you're more likely to win a race or a match than if your body is overloaded with adrenalin. Even for you and me, exercising in a relaxed and focused manner will make us fitter than gritting our teeth and slogging at it.

I exercise for an hour or so each day, and I try to meditate for most of that time. At the gym, I often work out with my eyes closed. I cut the past and future adrift and escape to the inner life of the body. Sometimes

I've got too much to think about and I can't focus as well as I would like, yet for me, to walk or go to the gym or do yoga or play golf are all wonderful opportunities to mentally relax.

FOUR SPOT-MEDITATIONS FOR EXERCISE

In the chapters that follow, I'll talk about three kinds of exercise: walking, weight work and yoga. They are all characterised by repetitive and often rhythmic movement, which makes them very suitable for spot-meditating.

If you normally do other kinds of exercise, you'll probably find ideas you can use. The instructions below easily adapt to the use of aerobic machines, or walking on the golf course or Tai Chi, for example. The competitive ball sports, on the other hand, generally demand bursts of adrenalin instead.

In each chapter, I'll present similar meditations adapted to the different activities of walking, gym work and yoga. The four meditations that apply to all of these are:

1. Focus on the Active Muscles

2. Deep Breathing

3. Soften the Inactive Muscles

4. Be Centred

These four exercises interact beautifully with each other. You could easily rotate through them in the space of a minute or so, to balance them. At any time, however, you should feel you are giving your emphasis to just one of them. Focusing on breathing as you pump iron or walk feels subtly different from focusing on the active muscles. Each exercise is quite distinct and is capable of infinite refinement.

In the chapter on walking, I present only the first three exercises although you could easily add the fourth as well. In the chapters on weight work and yoga, I also add in some extras that you've already learnt:

1. Stop before you start

2. Start consciously

3. Breathe through the muscles

32

Conscious Walking

The three exercises in this chapter are more systematic ways of doing the **Walk Comfortably meditation from Chapter 13.** They all invite you to be fully conscious of how you walk, and to feel your body from inside. In the first, you tune into the active muscles. In the second, you focus on deep, relaxed breathing and in the third, you scan the body and soften the inactive muscles. These meditations are best suited to longer, uninterrupted walks, and they can easily be adapted to running, swimming and using aerobic machines.

These exercises all support each other. You could easily go through them as a sequence on a single occasion, and you may occasionally feel as if you are doing them all simultaneously. After all, you can't focus on the active muscles while being completely oblivious to your breath or the rest of the body. However, try to resist the temptation to blur these exercises together. The rewards will be greater if you give priority to one at a time.

28. The Active Muscles

Sigh two or three times and start walking.

Focus on the active muscles in turn:

buttocks, thighs, calves…

Make good contact with each place.

Let go the unnecessary tension.

Feel the movement become smooth and flowing.

Breathe in a deep and relaxed fashion.

COMMENTARY

As you walk, certain muscles become more active than others. The buttock and thigh muscles are working quite hard, while the muscles in the arms and shoulders and face can remain quite loose and floppy. You don't go any faster if you clench your jaw or your fists.

In this meditation, you go 'inside the action' and mentally highlight the active muscles. It usually takes a few seconds or a minute to fully contact the movement in the buttocks, for example. You'll know you're there when you feel the movement become more smooth, flowing and efficient.

Then you gently scan through the other active muscles in turn, repeating the process. You can go to the front and back of the thighs, the knees, the calves and ankles. If you're short of time, then focusing on buttocks and thighs is quite sufficient.

You can make this meditation more sophisticated by going through the five stages described in Part Three. By focusing on the thighs, for example, you are effectively 'Naming the Action'. Then you notice the 'Stops and Starts' – the turnaround points with each step. Then you aim to 'Get inside the Action', to make it 'Smooth and Flowing' and to do it at exactly 'The Right Speed'.

This kind of deep focus will utterly change the quality of the exercise and your state of mind. Time slows down and almost stops. The outer world and all its concerns fall away as you escape into the vitality of your body.

Smooth, flowing movement...

29. Deep Breathing

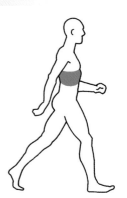

Sigh a few times and let the breath relax.

Breathe consciously from low in the body.

Keep the chest inactive.

Think 'out-in' as you breathe.

Make sure the out-breath is soft and loose.

Wait for the new breath to come when it wants to.

Enjoy the slow, deep, smooth rhythm of this:

energetic in-breaths, but soft and loose out-breaths.

'Breathe through' the active muscles.

Soften the inactive muscles.

COMMENTARY

I've already talked about Deep Breathing in Chapter 14, but let me remind you of the key points. A deep breath, though energetic, should still be a relaxed breath. You let the out-breath go fully, which makes it longer than the in-breath. You emphasise breathing from low in the body rather than from the chest. And even if you are running, the breathing should still feel fairly slow and loose, rather than abrupt and jerky.

Deep breathing can open up your posture beautifully. You can enhance this effect by focusing on different parts of the breathing mechanism in turn – sides, front, back. If you tune into the side ribs, for example, you'll find they soon move more freely and fully. You'll feel a similar effect if you focus on the diaphragm or the front of your abdomen.

30. Soften The Inactive Muscles

As you walk, tune into the active muscles.

Make the breathing deep and relaxed.

Now soften the inactive muscles.

Check out the face, the throat, the shoulders,

the wrists, the fingertips, the knees, the ankles, the toes.

Gently 'breathe through' them.

Scan at random or systematically up or down.

COMMENTARY

Certain muscles need to be activated when we walk, but not all of them. Unfortunately, adrenalin and anxiety are not specific in their effect: they make all the muscles tight, including those that don't need to be.

A student of mine who runs marathons told me his teacher used to say, 'Think floppy. Be a rag doll', before a race. Once he started running, the active muscles would kick in immediately but it would have been counterproductive to have tight shoulder and face muscles as well. In fact, you often see sportsmen shaking out their hands and feet, or rotating their heads, before a match or a race, to make sure they stay loose.

There are two ways to do this exercise. If you're on a long walk, it is best to establish good walking and deep breathing first. Only then would you scan the body and loosen the inactive muscles. Alternatively you could check for tension as soon as you start walking. You could scan systematically from top to bottom, as in Chapter 9, or you could move at random as tensions become obvious. Are you scrunching your eyes or your forehead? Are your shoulders swinging easily, and are the hands tight? Check out the fingers, the knees, the toes…

33

Pumping Iron

Many people feel relaxed in body and mind after a workout at the gym, but not all. Some people read magazines, watch TV, think about their day or generally space out — you couldn't say they were meditating. Some people grunt and slog, striving to maximise their muscle tone, and get a true 'gym body'. Others go to discuss shares and property, or to pick up their next girlfriend or boyfriend. So how do you meditate at the gym?

Let me speak for myself. The whole time I'm at the gym, I try to be as focused and relaxed as I possibly can. From the moment I get out of my car to the moment I return to it, I do scores of little meditations. Walking down the corridor, getting changed, going to the toilet, having a drink of water all have clear beginnings and ends, and I try to do each of these activities in a smooth, unhurried fashion.

In the gym itself I usually spend an equal amount of time on aerobic work, weight work and stretching. In this chapter, I'll talk about weight work. I'll explain stretching in the next chapter, and what I've already said about walking meditations also applies to aerobic work in the gym.

Weight work, or 'pumping iron', usually consists of dozens of short exercises, each of which you can easily turn into a spot-meditation. You sit at machines which enable you to push or pull weights up or down or sideways. We can call each push or pull a 'stroke', and people normally do a 'set' of a certain number of strokes.

Personally I don't count the repetitions. Instead I listen to my body and I do only the number of strokes that feel right on that day. I make sure my breathing is loose and relaxed, and I stop when it gets strained, which ensures that I work to my comfortable limit but no more.

I take my body to the gym the way you take a dog for a walk. You don't have to exercise your dog to the point of exhaustion each day, and neither do you have to flog your body. All it needs is a good romp. A dog likes to run around but it also knows when to slow down and rest. It doesn't tell itself, as humans do, "I'll stop running when I reach that tree in the distance".

I find that listening to my body in this way works beautifully for me. Those moments when I'm totally attuned to myself and doing an exercise perfectly are almost ecstatic. I can feel my body saying, "Thank you. I love this. It's exactly what I need." I also feel relaxed and energised when I walk out of the gym rather than exhausted.

The first exercise below – Pumping Iron – is a composite of everything I do when I work a machine. As you will see, most of the instructions below are meditations in their own right that I've already described in earlier chapters. In the commentary, I'll first explain how they work together, and then I'll explain them individually.

31. Pumping Iron

Breathe out and stop before you start.

Start consciously.

Focus on the active muscles.

Look for smooth, flowing movement.

Breathe deeply.

Soften the inactive muscles.

Feel centred and mentally still

while you pump.

Stop consciously.

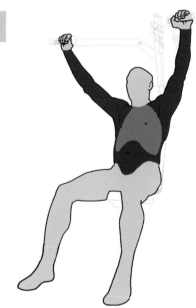

COMMENTARY

Even though a set may last only a minute, it still goes through several stages. I punctuate these stages using key words, as I describe below. Sometimes, it all flows together beautifully. I feel centred, mentally still and focused on the working muscles. I'm breathing easily, and the stroke is the ideal speed and length. The whole sequence feels like a perfectly balanced inner dance between my body and the machine.

In practice, I can't do justice to all of these spot-meditations in a single set, so I usually give priority to just one of them. As a result, when I focus primarily on my breath, I become slightly less attuned to the muscle movement. Similarly, when I look for that deep stillness in my centre of gravity, the breathing and the muscular movements become secondary. Let me now describe some of those spot-meditations in more detail.

32. Stop before you start

As you move to a new machine, sigh deeply.

When you sit down, breathe out and stop.

Wait for that pause between the breaths.

Feel your body become firm and still.

Start the action consciously.

COMMENTARY

During a set, certain muscles become tense, which is what 'toning' actually means. Pumping weights takes effort and oxygen, so you're likely to be breathing hard after a set, and certain muscles will have been pushed to their limits.

If you're not careful, those muscles can lock into place and stay tense long after the exercise is over. You may also forget to breathe. Gym instructors may have told you that you need to rest between sets to let the muscles soften. Many people, however, spend their whole hour at the gym tightening each muscle group in turn and holding them tight throughout.

So as you move to a new machine, sigh consciously two or three times until you feel a good, long pause at the end of the breath. You can even rest for longer, and deliberately 'breathe through' the muscles that you've just been working to help them soften. When you feel as centred and still as you want to be, then consciously start the next set.

33. The Active Muscles

Close your eyes and start the repetitions.

'Get inside' the active muscles.

Explore the movement in detail.

Feel it become smooth and economical.

Imagine you're 'breathing through' the muscles.

Make the stroke the right length and speed.

Notice when it is right to stop.

Stop consciously, breathe deeply and sigh.

COMMENTARY

As you start, tune into the exact muscles used for that particular machine. You'll find one region in the shoulders or arms or thighs or back that is particularly active. Mentally isolate these muscles and feel them solidly supported by the core of your body.

Because focusing naturally highlights what you focus on, you'll soon feel that part of the body in more detail. Those muscles may seem to light up from inside, while the rest of your body drops back into shadow. Let the active muscles work hard, but make sure the inactive muscles and your breathing remain soft.

As you 'get inside' the movement, it soon becomes more smooth and efficient. You will be using just the right muscles and the right amount of energy that the exercise requires. If, on the other hand, you're pumping mechanically with your mind elsewhere, it's easy to overreach and to activate muscles that are irrelevant to that particular exercise.

Notice when the movement starts feeling strained or grabby, and realise that it is now time to stop. Don't let the weights crash back to their resting position. Gently and deliberately put them down. To stop smoothly and consciously is part of the exercise.

34. Deep Breathing

Start working the weights but focus on the breath.

Breathe deeply and let the out-breath go completely.

Let the breath take priority:

fit the strokes around the breathing.

When the breath becomes strained, stop the exercise.

COMMENTARY

Don't forget to breathe just because pumping iron can be strenuous. People frequently hold their breaths or pant right through a set, and that's not relaxing at all. You can tell when they do this because they usually let go with an explosive sigh afterwards.

In this exercise, you make your breathing both deep and relaxed as you work. Deep, lower body breathing increases your lung capacity so you actually get the oxygen you need. Relaxed breathing means you also let the breath go fully. Even if you are working strenuously, you can still let the out-breath be soft and loose with a slight pause at the end.

Some machines open the chest in such a way that it makes sense to co-ordinate a single breath with a single stroke. However this is unnecessary with most machines, so I give priority to the breath and let the strokes take care of themselves.

If you habitually count repetitions and co-ordinate breaths and strokes, your breathing won't relax fully. A relaxed breath has a long, loose out-breath, and this rarely fits the equal in-out rhythm of the strokes. A deep breath also tends to be much longer than an individual stroke, and you'd have to chop it off or stretch it out to make it fit. When people count their repetitions, they usually co-ordinate breaths and strokes. I do neither because I find they interfere with the organic rhythm of deep, relaxed breathing.

35. Be Centred

Stop before you start.

Sink into your centre of gravity.

Feel the core of your body is strong and stable.

Start consciously.

Work the weights but keep your attention centred.

Breathe deeply and keep the body soft.

Imagine a 'straight' line of energy from your centre of gravity into the active muscles.

Notice if you start to strain or 'wobble'.

COMMENTARY

When you're doing an exercise well, you'll feel in touch with the active muscles, your breath and your whole body all at once. It is a subtle feeling, but you'll know when you've got it. You will especially notice your centre of gravity, which is that point of balance in your belly that holds it all together. Teachers of the martial arts say that all movement should originate from that place. A punch that comes from the belly is much stronger than one that simply comes from the shoulder.

If you primarily focus on your centre of gravity your mind can become very still. That inner place, deep in the body, may not be moving at all, even though your arms or legs may be quite busy around it. When you get that inner feeling, the core of your body feels strong and unmoving throughout the whole stroke. The technical term for this is 'core stability'.

Once you feel centred, try to feel a 'straight' line of energy from your centre of gravity through your body into the active muscles, and then into the weights. Because pumping iron is strenuous, it's easy to lose that core stability. That's when you'll overreach and feel strain. You'll also feel a wobble in that invisible line of energy from your centre of gravity into the active muscles. If you can't re-establish it, then stop.

After you complete the set, you can continue to remain centred as you move to the next machine.

USING KEY WORDS AS TRIGGERS

Any particular exercise consists of successive stages, and it is helpful to use key words and phrases to remind you exactly what you are doing at any point. I personally use them as triggers as I shift from one stage to another. Once you know what a phrase means, you can usually contract it to a single word. I would suggest the following:

Stop before you start, or simply: 'Stop'

Start consciously, or simply: 'Start'

Focus on the active muscles, or simply: 'Muscles'

Deep, relaxed breathing, or simply: 'Breathe'

Soften the inactive muscles, or simply: 'Soften'

The centre of gravity, or simply: 'Centre'

Breathe out and stop, or simply: 'Stop'.

Key Words
Stop
Start
Muscles
Breathe
Soften
Centre
Stop

Yoga

Meditation has come to the West largely from Buddhism and yoga. Buddhism, however, as an old-time religion, is much more than meditation alone, and yoga is often reduced to a form of physical fitness no more spiritual than weight-training. In fact, if you go to a local Buddhist group or yoga class you may learn virtually nothing about meditation, though the word frequently floats through the air to lend a certain authority.

In yoga classes, 'meditation' often means little more than doing breathing exercises, or falling asleep on the floor at the end of a class. This is a dreadful waste. Yoga has the potential to be one of the best possible combinations of physical exercise and mental training.

So why are yoga and stretching exercises so useful? Yoga is a perfect antidote to one of the major effects of stress: tight muscles. Adrenalin tightens hundreds of muscles throughout the body, and yoga reverses this effect by stretching them through many ingenious poses. Of course, if you relax the body, the mind also settles down.

Yoga uses the breath well. Quite apart from its specific breath exercises, it emphasises deep, slow breathing while in the poses. This dismantles the habit of tight, chest breathing that is so characteristic of anxious people, and opens the muscles and joints to a degree that non-yogis cannot imagine.

If you do yoga mechanically, it's just a physical exercise and nowhere near as useful as it might be. If your mind is anxious and tense, your body will be too, and your attempts to stretch the muscles will battle against the anxious body's instinct to hold them in contraction.

Yoga can be a wonderful meditation if you pay moment-to-moment attention to what you are doing. Can you move consciously and smoothly into the pose? Is your breathing deep and easy? Can you mentally rest in your centre of gravity, feeling the muscles loosen around you? Do you exit the pose consciously? Can you breathe out fully and return to a point of stillness before the next pose?

If you do all this, your body will become supple and strong and you'll also relax mentally. You'll be calm and attentive, and fully in the present. You won't need to go to a desert island or mountain top to unwind. You can find your sanctuary within the boundaries of your own body.

36. Yoga

Breathe out and stop before you start.

Start consciously.

Focus on the active muscles

(some tensing, some stretching).

Breathe deeply.

Find your centre of gravity.

Relax further into the stretch.

Soften the inactive muscles.

Stop consciously.

Breathe out and stop before the next pose.

COMMENTARY

You might have realised that the instructions above are almost identical to those for Pumping Iron, with just a couple of changes. In fact, the core instructions for walking, yoga and weight work are all the same:

1. Focus on the active muscles

2. Breathe deeply

3. Soften the inactive muscles

4. Be centred

If you simply remember these four instructions (or spot-meditations actually), plus the idea of Stopping before you Start, you have nearly all you need for most forms of exercise. Nonetheless, you apply them in a particular way with yoga as I'll explain below.

FOCUS ON THE ACTIVE MUSCLES

The many poses are designed to stretch, and therefore relax, individual muscle groups in turn. Some poses, such as forward bends, are relatively passive, and the whole body can sink into the exercise. Others, such as the standing poses, are more active, and involve some muscles tensing up while others relax.

So relaxation means at least two different things in yoga. Firstly, you relax certain muscles by persuading them to stretch. Secondly, when other muscles need to be tense, you tense them only to the degree necessary.

As you enter the pose, notice which muscles are active. Tune into both those that are stretching and those that are tensing, until you can feel the sensations in detail. As your awareness becomes sharper, you'll soon notice both kinds of muscles working more efficiently and doing what they should be doing.

DEEP, RELAXED BREATHING

In every pose, breathe as easily and deeply as you can. Because yoga takes a certain effort, people are inclined to hold their breath or breathe spasmodically throughout the pose. When they can hold it no longer, they burst out of the pose, gasping with the strain. Furthermore, some poses twist or compress the torso, making it difficult to breathe.

Yet even in the strangest poses, we still have a certain freedom to breathe as gently as is possible. Deep, relaxed breathing has an amazing ripple effect throughout the body, helping the muscles you are trying to stretch to free up even more. Conversely, you can't expect muscles to relax much if you're holding your breath: the body doesn't operate that way.

BE CENTRED

When the pose feels firm, it is as if your mind spreads equally throughout your whole body, illuminating it from inside. You also become very conscious of your centre of gravity, which is that firm, stable place in your belly that holds the rest of your body in balance. When your posture and breathing are well established, let your mind become still. Close your eyes and sink into your centre of gravity.

The Indian sage Patanjali over 2000 years ago put this concept into a useful aphorism. He said 'The pose should be steady and comfortable'. The word 'steady' means to be firm, strong and balanced in the pose – much the same as what I referred to as 'core stability' in the last chapter. The word 'comfortable' means that you are breathing deeply and easily, with no unnecessary effort. The Sanskrit word for 'comfortable' also refers to the pleasure you feel as the muscles stretch and more life flows through the body.

SOFTEN THE INACTIVE MUSCLES

When you're firm and comfortable in the pose, and breathing easily, then focus on those muscles that are stretching. You can't force them to stretch but you can invite them to let go a little more. Notice any subtle resistance and gently breathe through it. If your breathing is soft and loose, it encourages the muscles to loosen also.

You're often so focused on just one set of muscles that you fail to notice what is happening elsewhere in the body. If you check, you may find unnecessary tensions in all kinds of strange places. While stretching your hamstrings, for example, you may also be screwing up your face or holding your neck tight. This doesn't help at all, so casually scan your whole body and soften the inactive muscles wherever you find them. You'll feel so much better when you do.

CONSCIOUSLY START AND STOP

A pose can take half a minute or more to establish. There can be a long transitional zone as you move your body into position and steady the pose. Beginners tend to miss this transition. They jump impatiently into the pose and only start to 'do their yoga' when they're there.

Good yogis, on the other hand, flow smoothly into the pose, constructing it with an inner awareness that is quite lovely to watch. Likewise, they gradually emerge from the pose at the end and return consciously to a balanced, still position. This gives them a seamless continuity as they move from one posture to another. They are fully 'there' every inch of the way.

You can do the same. As you emerge from the pose and return to standing, expand your whole body. Stand tall. If you're sitting, sit up straight and open your torso. Breathe deeply, two or three times at least. Wait for the pause between the breaths to be full and spacious before you move into the next pose.

SUMMARY

A yoga pose is complex and consists of many successive stages. Just as with pumping iron, it is helpful to use key words and phrases to remind you exactly what you are doing at any point. As I mentioned in the last chapter, once you know what a phrase means, you can usually contract it into a single word. I would suggest the following:

Key Words
Stop
Start
Muscles
Breathe
Soften
Centre
Stop

Stop before you start, or simply: 'Stop'

Start consciously, or simply: 'Start'

Focus on the active muscles, or simply: 'Muscles'

Deep, relaxed breathing, or simply: 'Breathe'

Soften the inactive muscles, or simply: 'Soften'

The centre of gravity, or simply: 'Centre'

Breathe out and stop, or simply: 'Stop'.

Or you could use Patanjali's aphorism:

'Firm and Comfortable'

Part Five

Putting It Together

35

Household Activities

Do you want to relax while doing the housework? You've now got many options. The exercises in Part One explained how to focus inwardly on your breath and your body while doing so. While you prepare food, you could sigh gently, saying 'relax' or 'let go' while you do so.

Part Two invited you to focus instead on the sensuality of the action. You could listen to the sounds you make as you prepare food, while saying 'sound' or 'listening'. Or you could simply try to 'be here', by tuning into whatever sight, sound, smell, or tactile sensation was catching your attention in that moment.

Part Three gave you further options. It explained how to 'do what you are doing' by naming the action ('cooking'), and noticing the stops and starts of the micro-actions. Alternatively, you could focus on the way you move, saying 'smooth, unhurried action', as you do so. Let me now give you examples of how it all works in practice.

AT THE KITCHEN SINK

Twenty years ago, I did a seven-month retreat, most of it in a tiny hut, high on a mountainside in the Southern Alps of New Zealand. I was alone all week, except for Wednesday, when I collected my food for the days ahead. I did sitting meditations for about nine hours a day, plus three or four hours of yoga and walking meditations.

Inevitably, the housework became infused with the spirit of meditation. I particularly looked forward to preparing my food. That kind of secluded lifestyle enhances sensory awareness, so making a meal became a little drama of sight and sound and smell and texture that I enjoyed enormously.

Nowadays, I will still do those 'kitchen sink' meditations while preparing food. Sometimes I focus on just one sense, such as sound. I deliberately listen to each sound I make: cutting the apple, putting the knife down, the squeal of the tap and the water running, the bowl scraping on the bench, a foot shuffle, the fridge door opening, the clang as I place something on a rack, and so on. I am aware of other sensations of course, but I highlight the sounds.

Alternatively, I notice input from any sense, while thinking the phrase 'Be Here'. Preparing food naturally moves your attention from sight to sound to texture to smell. So I notice the texture of the knife, fruit, water, the door handle. Or the glistening skin of a capsicum, or patterns of light and shadow, a stain on the bench. Or the sensations in my arm as I lift something or put it down. It can be surprisingly pleasant!

HAVING A CUP OF TEA

Making a cup of tea is an excellent way to 'do what you are doing'. I find the actual making of the tea works better than the drinking of it. Making tea consists of many small, delicate movements, with the occasional short pause between them.

Making a cup of tea has clear boundaries. It starts with the intention and finishes when you put the tea where you're about to drink it. It's an activity that doesn't just fade away into something else and, because it only takes two or three minutes, you can give it more complete attention than you would to a longer activity. As I've said before: high quality focus for short duration gives the best results.

When making a cup of tea, I first relax my breath and soften my body. Then I 'get into the action'. I notice the stops and starts of the micro-actions, and develop a smooth, unhurried quality of movement. I also notice the sounds, sights and smells but I don't highlight them as in the 'kitchen sink' meditation above.

KEY WORDS
Sigh gently
Let go
Soften the body
Be sensual
Just listen
Just look
Just be here
Name the action
Stops and starts
Flowing movement

Tea in fact has a long connection with Zen meditation. As the guest in the Japanese tea ceremony, you patiently watch each movement of the tea-maker. You hear the sounds, watch the steam, enjoy the decorations in the room, feel and look at the bowl, taste the tea and feel yourself swallowing. You become calm by focusing on one small detail after another.

The ceremony was cultivated in medieval times to create a tranquil space in a violent world, and traditionally occurred in a specially designed teahouse in a garden. The samurai warrior caste would symbolically leave their swords, and their warlike nature, outside the hut to enter that space.

You can do exactly the same in your own kitchen. If you want to escape the warfare of the modern world, turn your back on it and make a cup of tea.

TAKE A SHOWER

I did my first ten-day retreat in 1975, and I had an epiphany on the third day: I had a shower. I went into the shabby cubicle at the old Catholic retreat centre in Auckland, New Zealand, and had a shower like I'd never had before.

Three days of meditation had made my mind very still and clear. Every sense was heightened, so when the water hit me, it was an explosion of delight. I felt my skin sing. The light and sounds were radiant and lovely, and textures exquisite. A shower had never felt so magical before and, at that moment, I knew that pleasure comes from inside. If my mind was clear, even the simplest things could be ecstatic (and I didn't need to be fabulously rich to buy happiness).

Nowadays, I similarly focus on the pure sensations of having a shower: the smell of soap, the sounds and texture of water, the warmth and skin response, the pleasurable bodily movements. I don't meditate on showering every time I shower, but it is an option I take up two or three times a week. I always notice how lovely it feels and consciously appreciate it. Hot water on demand – what a luxury in the history of mankind! It also confirms the basic formula: if you want to be relaxed, be more sensual.

GETTING DRESSED

Showering naturally leads into another meditation: getting dressed and getting ready to go out. If you think I'm inventing this as an easy option for busy Westerners, you've got it wrong.

I'll let you into a secret. The Buddha was no laid back hippie. He was a bit of a fusspot, and he insisted his monks always look neat and tidy when they went out. He said that if they were sloppy in their dress and behaviour, it would reflect badly on him and his reputation. He was like a headmaster who wanted his boys to have their shirts tucked in and their hair combed when they went through town.

Since he had a lifelong passion for both making rules and inventing meditation practices, he asked his monks to meditate on getting dressed. While monks are sitting, their robes get somewhat slack. As they stand up, they are required to spend quite some time making sure their robes hang properly and look nice. You'll notice monks doing this deliberately even now, in the 21st century. It's in their rules of monastic etiquette.

If your husband, therefore, is annoyed about the time you take in front of your make-up mirror, just tell him you're doing an ancient Buddhist meditation adapted to the modern world. If he goes off in a huff, accuse him of religious insensitivity!

OTHER POSSIBLE ACTIVITIES

After an hour or two of desk work, I like to take a break. Once or twice a day, I simply potter around for five or ten minutes, tidying up. There are always bits of paper or clothing where they shouldn't be, a few unwashed dishes, or food that needs to be put away. I enjoy the fact that my body is moving and breathing more easily – it's a relief to get out of the chair. I usually focus on deep, relaxed breathing while I move. I enjoy the bending and touching and lifting and placing, and I try to do it all in a smooth, unhurried fashion.

There are dozens of household activities you can meditate on: weeding or planting; washing the baby or the car; simple handyman tasks; carrying out the garbage or hanging out the washing; cleaning the kitchen; doing the ironing or making the bed. Meditating can make these activities more pleasant or at least reduce their drudgery. We will be picking up socks all our lives, so we might as well do it in a relaxed fashion.

The easiest kinds of household activities to turn into meditations are those that are relatively short and have clear start and finish points. The simplicity is the key. It is as if you leave behind the intellectual demands of your life in the 21st century and revert to the simple life of a Victorian servant. You can see how people who are house-proud can get a certain quiet satisfaction out of cleaning up the kitchen properly. We can all do the dishes, but to do them in a relaxed, contented fashion is another matter.

36 Going To The Toilet

It's quite relaxing to go to the toilet. At least one sphincter has to relax completely or it's not worth going there at all. When you let one muscle go, you'll find that others will relax in sympathy. Furthermore, the toilet may be the only place all day where no one will disturb you. You can always grab a few extra seconds there and no one will complain.

The Buddha recommended urinating as a meditation object 2500 years ago. A psychologist friend told me that he goes to the toilet in the five minutes between clients, and lets *everything* go along with the urine. He gets so relaxed in those few seconds he says he can barely hold his balance.

In Western literature, it is surprising how often the toilet is regarded as a suitable place for deep thought. You sit down and settle into your body. You relax and wait, and survey the state of the nation. Not surprisingly, bright ideas can arise and you feel relaxed for minutes afterwards. An excellent meditation!

37. Going To The Toilet

As you approach the toilet, sigh in anticipation.

Get out of your head and into your body.

Feel the pressure in your bladder.

As you urinate, close your eyes and sigh deeply.

Feel your whole body loosening in sympathy.

Don't hurry to finish. No one will disturb you.

Enjoy that space after the last drop: nothing to do.

Walk away with a smile on your face.

37

Drive Safely

In my early years as a teacher, I was afraid that students who meditated while driving would relax too much and crash. So I told them firmly: "Don't meditate while driving! A few seconds asleep at the wheel is enough to kill you." I would add that an estimated 20% of fatalities are caused by drivers who fall asleep.

I found that many of my students ignored my portentous warnings. Once they learnt to spot-meditate, they soon tried it out in the car. Rather than killing themselves however, they usually reported they were driving more safely, getting less speeding tickets and being more tolerant towards the idiots on the road. Since they were doing it anyway, I decided to teach them how to do it safely.

HOW TO KILL YOURSELF WHILE DRIVING

It is quite possible to meditate in a dangerous way when you drive. One student told me he was so shocked by a certain experience, he'd never try it again. He realised that by focusing on his breath while driving, he'd slipped into dreamland for a few hundred yards before he came to.

That's how you kill yourself. When you're driving, don't focus *inwardly* on the breath, and don't focus on just one thing. You need to focus *outwardly* on the activity of driving itself, which is a much more complex array of actions and sensations.

If you focus for too long on any one thing, even an external object such as a cloud or the marks on the road, everything else slips into the margins. Focusing on one thing while driving will certainly relax you, but will you still be there at the next intersection?

So scan constantly when you drive. Focus on many things in succession. Notice the traffic, the sky, the scenery. Be present. Go for a wide angle awareness rather than pinpoint focus. Don't leave the outside world behind. Notice your breathing and muscle tension, but don't let your mind settle there as you would in a normal sitting meditation. And wake yourself up quickly when you realise you're falling asleep. Meditating even for a few seconds can make you relax far more deeply than you realise.

When you drive, you can easily become drowsy, even without meditating. You may notice a momentary blankness, or the eyes want to close, or the head bobs. These are clear signs that you need to wake up if you want to stay alive. If you can't pull over and have a few minutes rest, at least open the window, breathe more deeply and consciously look around you.

38. Drive Safely

Consciously get into the car.

Breathe out and stop before you start.

Drive away consciously.

Tune into the road conditions.

Notice the traffic, the sky, the scenery.

Be present.

Know what you are doing at this moment.

Make your actions smooth and flowing.

Drive at the right speed.

Consciously stop and start.

Consciously slow down and speed up.

Be more alert at corners and intersections.

Soften the breath and the body,

but without taking your attention off the road.

Focus primarily on the body only when the car is still.

Watch for the first signs of drowsiness.

Take immediate action to wake yourself up.

COMMENTARY

CONSCIOUSLY GET INTO THE CAR AND DRIVE AWAY

It's quite possible to drive across town while lost in reverie, not noticing or remembering a single detail of the journey. Most people can even get home if they're drunk or stoned or in the first stages of dementia. It is scary to realise how absent people are when they drive. If you check, you may find you're hardly ever fully present driving down this street at this time towards this intersection.

For my own safety, I at least try to start driving consciously. The exercise goes like this: I breathe deeply as I approach the car door. I hear the sounds I make as I open the door, and notice the tactile sensations. I throw my bag on the adjacent seat and sit down. I consciously adjust my position in the seat. I put the key in the ignition and turn it on, while also putting the car into gear. I take the hand brake off while also pulling across the seat belt. I slot in the seat belt and notice the end of that action before driving away.

> **To drive safely:**
>
> **Don't focus inwardly:**
> focus outwardly, on the activity of driving.
>
> **Don't focus on just one thing:**
> scan gently from one thing to another.

In other words, I try to 'do what I'm doing' and to move in a smooth, unhurried fashion. This doesn't slow me down at all, yet there is a clear sign when I've failed to be present: I drive away before I put the seat belt on. I find myself pulling out into traffic and changing gears while trying to sort out the seat belt as well. Not a good idea.

DON'T HURRY: DRIVE AT THE RIGHT SPEED

I've suggested that there is a right speed – not too fast nor too slow – for every activity. Worry and adrenalin make us hurry, which is often quite useless when we drive. Racing for the lights, scrambling for the most advantageous lane, speeding between intersections and waiting impatiently when we have to wait, are unlikely to get us to our destination even a minute sooner. And at what price to our nerves?

While you drive, think 'the right speed', or 'smooth, unhurried action.' Drive at just the right speed as you accelerate away from the lights, as you go around a corner, as you drive down the road, as you slow down. There is also a right speed for the way you change gears and turn the steering wheel. Also obey the law. If you drive more than five km above the speed limit, you're bound to be somewhat anxious about getting caught.

Drive consciously, but don't be hypervigilant the whole time. On an open road or an empty street you can relax and enjoy your surroundings more. That's when it is safer to loosen up the breath and the body. But safe driving also requires anticipation. When you approach an intersection or a corner, I suggest you name it – 'intersection' or 'corner' – to remind yourself to be more alert.

At least he died peacefully…

38

Red Light

I **took many radio interviews when my book** *Teach Yourself* *to Meditate* **came out in 1993.** The interviewers were fascinated by the idea that you could relax in the forty-five seconds you were stuck at a red light. In fact, a television team invited me to fly across the continent to Melbourne so I could demonstrate.

A team of eight with a back-up truck met me at the airport. The car had a camera mounted on the bonnet, pointing to the driver's seat. It was a grey winter's day, so the technicians had put bright lights within the car itself, shining up on my face. I drove off into rush hour traffic, late on a dismal Friday afternoon, to demonstrate the Red Light meditation. It wasn't easy.

I suggest you regard any red light as a visual meditation instruction. It reminds you to breathe out and stop before you start. The car has stopped. Why don't you stop as well? It is not hard to drop the thoughts temporarily and just be here. At the very least, sigh two or three times at a red light, not out of exasperation but for the sheer pleasure of letting everything go.

This exercise works best if you are running late and the traffic lights turn red as you approach.

39. The Red Light

Smile. You have been given a whole minute
to stop and do nothing.
Relax. Sigh two or three times.
Settle back into the seat.
Scan your body for tension.
Soften your face. Yawn.
How are you holding the steering wheel?
Let your shoulders drop. Let your belly soften.
Let the breath go completely.
Be present. Look around you slowly.
Notice the scenery, the traffic, the sky.
This exercise finishes when the lights turn green.
Now devote all your attention to the task at hand:
Drive safely, and look forward to the next red light.

39

When You Have To Wait

Nowadays we're always waiting. For buses or trains, in traffic jams, at red lights, for children outside schools, in supermarket or bank queues. We wait for the TV ads to pass, for the boring lecture or meeting to be over, for the meal to cook. We wait to fall asleep and, if we wake early, we wait till it's time to get up. One student said, "I fly about twenty-five times a month. I waste whole days in airport lounges and planes and hotels and taxis." We're all so busy and yet we waste so much time unable to do anything.

It doesn't need to be this way. Don't waste that waiting time. You could consciously relax in nearly all the situations above. Standing in a supermarket queue could be your best chance all day to go inwards, to take stock and unwind. The more stressed you are, the more rapidly you benefit from a spot-meditation. A few deep breaths and a change of attitude will bring you down from the stress zone within seconds.

Waiting usually makes us frustrated and irritable. We grind our teeth and fume, and our blood pressure and metabolic rate rise. We use the opportunity to get even more tense than we are already, and burn a huge amount of energy while doing nothing at all. Rather than getting frustrated in a queue, just say to yourself, "Wonderful! I've now got a chance to slow down and relax. I'll drop some of that tension I've been carrying all day."

40. Stand and wait

When in a queue, sigh two or three times.

Loosen up your posture.

Settle your eyes on one thing,

and let your gaze soften.

Sigh gently, or say 'let go' as you breathe.

Soften your body.

Scan systematically over seven breaths, or casually loosen the obvious tensions.

Notice how soft, heavy and still your body can become while you stand.

COMMENTARY

So how do you meditate while standing? First, you may discover that it is impossible to stand still. We really need a third leg to be perfectly immobile. We all naturally sway and shuffle around when we stand, and you can use that movement to loosen up your body without drawing attention to yourself.

While in a queue, settle your eyes gently on something in front of you. The shoulder of the next person will do just fine. When you've anchored your gaze, then let the eyes soften, so they're almost out of focus. Your peripheral vision will still tell you what's happening around you and when to move forward.

Now loosen up your posture and breathing. Take two or three deep breaths and soften your body. If you have the time, scan the body over seven breaths. Alternatively you could focus on deep, relaxed breathing, while resting your mind in your centre of gravity. You could even focus on something visual and gently examine it.

It's good to silently talk to yourself so you don't get distracted. If you're looking at a blue object, then say the word 'blue', as you breathe. If you're scanning the body, then count the stages. If you're simply focused on the breath, then say 'let go' as you breathe. Childish as these devices seem, they all remind you what you are doing and keep you on track. When you get distracted, the words often continue of their own momentum and call you back.

40

How to Fall Asleep

If you're feeling tired, even a minute or two at the edge of sleep will refresh you. Sleep researchers have found that you don't actually have to fall asleep to work off some of your 'sleep debt'. You can benefit from just touching the threshold.

If you feel exhausted during the day, you hardly need a technique to help you relax. You just give yourself permission to collapse, while staying in an upright position to keep control. Even in a public place, you can relax deeply with the confidence that you won't snooze off and start drooling. In those circumstances, you rarely fall asleep totally. Your guardian angel is looking out for you, so don't feel shy about relaxing as deeply as you need to.

Go and sit in the toilet for a couple of minutes. Close your eyes when on public transport and disappear. When I was at school, I used to sit in my car at lunchtime. You'll be amazed at how quickly you can relax to the edge of sleep if you give yourself half a chance.

41. The Mini-Nap

When you're exhausted, let yourself fall asleep.

Find a place where you can sit and close your eyes.

Say the words, 'Let go', or 'sleep', as you breathe.

Let your body feel heavy and soft.

Go to the edge, but don't fall off the chair.

Enjoy that dark, inward feeling.

Come out when you have to, and get moving again.

42. Falling asleep

Lying on your back is usually best.

Choose your meditation:

breath, bodyscan, sounds or music.

Focus as intently as you can,

even if you constantly lose focus.

Go for detail.

Even a minute of sharp focus can put you to sleep.

If you remain awake, tell yourself:

'At least, I'm relaxing'.

COMMENTARY

TO FALL ASLEEP, FOCUS INTENTLY

Insomnia is a huge problem in our speedy and over-bright world. It's both a cause and an effect of stress, depression and many lifestyle illnesses. I suspect most of our misery and sickness would vanish if we could simply sleep as well as people did a hundred years ago. (They averaged two hours a night more than we do now).

Often the only time people find to meditate is when they're in bed, trying to fall asleep. In fact, it's a perfect opportunity. I often meditate to go to sleep, or to put myself back to sleep when I wake at night. It rarely takes more than a minute or two.

When in bed, our thoughts tend to ramble unproductively, but they can still keep us awake. Paradoxically, the way to fall asleep is to focus intently, and in fact to make the mind as sharp as possible. This is the only way to escape the rambling thoughts. You can't waffle your way back to sleep.

Forget about counting sheep. Counting the breaths or scanning the body is so much better, but don't be lazy about it. Don't lose the count. Check that you actually feel the end and start of each breath. You need this kind of precise focus to escape the thoughts that are keeping you awake. Remember that deep, sharp focus automatically relaxes you: it is the royal road into the trance states. If you're at all sleepy and your mind becomes very focused, it is almost impossible to stay awake while lying in bed.

Other options while in bed include listening to the sounds around you, or switching on a piece of music. I have my stereo remote on my bedside table so if I wake in the night, I can switch on music without even turning on the light.

Even if meditation fails to put us back to sleep, the benefits can be huge. If we lie awake and think all night, we burn a lot of energy and get up in the morning frustrated and exhausted. If, on the other hand, we meditate through the small hours, we will rest and conserve energy, though still awake. We're also more likely to dip in and out of sleep for a few minutes here and there.

While not ideal, this is vastly preferable to fretting all night. One of my students was in such pain that he rarely slept for more than half an hour at a time. He found that although he still remained awake much of the night, by meditating in the small hours, he rested far more deeply than he had for years. This gave him much more energy to run his two businesses during the day. He was delighted with the results of his night-time meditations.

41

Final Words

Congratulations! You've reached the end of this book, but what do you do now? Meditation is easy to understand but, because it is a skill, you only get good at it if you practise. If you want satisfaction, I suggest you ask yourself three questions:

Why do I want to meditate?

How important is it to me?

How much will I need to practise?

Of course, none of us feel we have time to do anything extra, so it is good to remind yourself that meditation is not an either/or. It doesn't need to interrupt your daily activities: it only interrupts the momentum of your thoughts. I have a busy life, but I still manage to spot-meditate one or two hours a day.

A few minutes a day will be sufficient if your goals are modest. Assuming that you meditate well, however, let me explain the results you can expect from a daily practice of ten minutes, or thirty minutes and even more.

HOW MUCH?

If you aim for a total of ten minutes a day, you will be able to relax quickly and consciously whenever you want to. You may not relax deeply, but results can be truly amazing for such a short investment of time. It only takes a minute to wind down your stress levels 20-30%, and you can stay relaxed for quite a while afterwards. If ten minutes seems possible, I suggest you work mainly with meditations 1-8. Just aim to consciously sigh, stop, scan the body and walk comfortably whenever possible, and see where that takes you.

It is quite possible to meditate for thirty minutes a day if you systematically include the times when you walk or exercise, or do simple household activities. Just think 'be here, be sensual, and do what you are doing'. You will learn how to stop the merry-go-round, to contact the sense world deeply, and to know exactly what you are doing and thinking and feeling. In time, your quality of life can change utterly. In fact, skilful spot-meditations can give you all the benefits of long meditations, except for the states of trance.

I commonly find, however, that people don't extract the full potential from short meditations unless they also get familiar with long ones (twenty minutes or more). Combining short and long ones will give you much better results than only doing one or the other. Spot-meditations naturally become longer as you get better at them but, if you want more direction, you can refer to my other book, *Do You Want to Meditate?*, or my CDs.

WHERE TO FROM HERE?

As you can tell, most of the exercises in this book come from Buddhism and Yoga. I am very grateful to those ancient yogis. I love these exercises immensely and they are fully integrated into my life, but I use them for some quite unspiritual purposes – enhancing sensual pleasure, for example. The Buddha would turn in his grave if he knew. On many important matters we don't see eye-to-eye.

So please don't take my love of meditation as an endorsement of Buddhism itself. The Buddha was an extreme ascetic. He said that the world was loathsome and life was utter misery (Not my experience). Sensual pleasures are repulsive, he said, and beware of women (I've failed). Love is just a recipe for misery (That's what he said!) If you want peace, then purge your mind of every emotion (That's what Nirvana entails). Demolish your sense of being an individual, and try to think like him (Can't do it and don't want to).

Of course Western Buddhist teachers usually take a softer line, and they do in fact salvage much that is useful from this grim tradition. There is no doubt that meditation itself is valuable but the question is: do you need Buddhism (or Yoga) at all? In those groups, you usually find meditation as a small part of a larger package: meditation + Buddhism, or meditation + Yoga. However it is quite easy to extract the meditation from the dogma with no great loss, and use it for your own purposes.

I personally feel that happiness comes from accepting yourself as an individual and following your own path. I find that the world, and the people in it, are profoundly beautiful, and I can't help loving them. These are common Western attitudes – they are not Buddhist at all – and yet meditation can greatly enhance them. Meditation, by cultivating a calm, focused mind, interacts well with Western psychology, philosophy and science, and has much to offer as we search for happiness and understanding. If you want your meditation as part of a package, I would suggest: meditation + Western culture.

Throughout this book, I've suggested that you imaginatively adapt this skill to your kind of life for your particular purposes. At a certain point you will know 'I've got it! This feels really good. And I can do it again and again in all circumstances.' Then you can throw away this book and confidently walk off on your own.

I can promise you that a healthy practice continues to blossom and bear fruit over the years. I may be wrong, but there seems to be no end to this road. You will never exhaust the possibilities if you let your imagination guide you. It is an amazing journey.

Thank You

Countless people have contributed to this little book. Most of the techniques here originated from the Buddha or the yogis of ancient times and I gratefully acknowledge my debt to them.

My students have contributed to this book without their realising it. Over the years, I've faced thousands of sick, stressed-out, anxious people who find relaxation a very alien concept. They have forced me to find explanations that they understand, and methods that work for them. Every good teacher is shaped by his students, and I appreciate what I have learnt from them.

I've published many books, but this is the first in which I have made full use of talented designers. It has been a delight working with John Cooper and Rozz Synnot from A Very Useful Design Service. They have been able to express in pictures, colour and design what I can only put into words. I greatly appreciate the passion and imagination they have put into this work – far beyond the call of duty. My thanks also go to the many anonymous photographers whose images we used.

Finally, I want to thank my girlfriend Susan, for her constant inspiration and for keeping my heart warm. She has contributed deeply to this book, and she even thought up the title. I dedicate *The 5-Minute Meditator* to her.

To Susan
with love

Index of Meditations

Iestablished Perth Meditation Centre in 1987 as a school for teaching meditation. Since then, I have taught forty to sixty courses annually, mostly of seven weeks' duration, and led scores of workshops and retreats. I also run many seminars and workshops for the corporate world, for universities and for government bodies. I'm often invited to teach in other cities and towns, and I see people privately.

I teach meditation solely as a technical skill for relaxation and mental clarity, on the assumption that these are extremely valuable in their own right. I've had a lifelong interest in psychology, philosophy and science, so I avoid using spiritual or New Age language that makes little sense to a rational Westerner like myself. In class, the students sit in a circle of chairs, not on the floor or lying down. I like my students to understand exactly what they are doing, and how it all works.

About a quarter of my students are referrals from doctors and psychologists. I see a lot of very sick and stressed people, and those who are heading that way. It still amazes me to see how rapidly their lives can improve if they meditate. I wrote my book *Meditation and Health*, (now out of print, but available in libraries), for their benefit.

I originally trained a few people to teach in my style. In recent years however, I've trained about forty people to use meditation in whatever way suits their occupation. Meditation combines well with therapy, health care, body work, personal growth and spiritual endeavours, and I like to see people in those fields making use of it. A few of my students now teach meditation as a secondary career.

www.perthmeditationcentre.com.au

DO YOU WANT TO MEDITATE?

I originally wrote this book in 1989 as notes for my students. I prefer to publish the book myself in Australia, because this allows me to revise it every few years, to keep it abreast of my teaching style. The fully revised fifth edition is due out in January 2006.

I've sold the book overseas to other publishers, particularly to Simon and Schuster, and Piatkus Books (UK). It has now sold 150,000 copies worldwide, been translated into ten languages and been pirated in at least two more.

The current edition of *Do You Want to Meditate?* describes both long and short meditations. In future, I'll use *The 5-Minute Meditator* to describe the short meditations, and I'll explain the longer meditations in the next edition of *Do You Want to Meditate?*

Longer meditations allow you to see your thoughts and feelings, and the workings of the mind, with great subtlety and understanding. They also lead to deep tranquility and physical health and are the pathway to the inner worlds. They help you cope with pain and sadness, and help you find beauty and meaning in a complicated world. Done with awareness, and used in conjunction with spot-meditations, they really can give you all the benefits traditionally associated with meditation.

Do You Want to Meditate? is the natural follow-on from *The 5-Minute Meditator.* Once you know how to do short meditations, you'll find they soon tend to become longer anyway. Long meditations have greater possibilities but also different challenges. This book explains how to get the most out of this very useful skill.

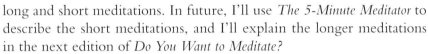

HOW TO MEDITATE

This set of four CDs is the companion to *Do You Want to Meditate?* It contains two and a half hours of mostly long guided meditations with subtle musical accompaniment, plus explanations. For years, I resisted putting out CDs because people often become reliant on them and a bit lazy, so I designed the meditations

on this set with a special aim in mind. They not only guide you: they also train you to eventually meditate without needing the CDs.

HOW MUCH?

The current prices for books and CDs are:

The 5-Minute Meditator	$25+$5 postage
Do You Want to Meditate?	$25+$5 postage
How to Meditate	$70+$5 postage

You can order these products by email, post or phone, and pay by credit card or cheque.

FIND OUT MORE

The website will always have up-to-date information on books, CDs and courses. Alternatively, you can contact us, and we will send you a current brochure.

Post:	PMC, Box 1019, Subiaco WA 6904, Australia
Location:	8/280 Hay St, Subiaco
Phone:	(08) 9381 4877
web:	www.perthmeditationcentre.com.au
email:	eric@perthmeditationcentre.com.au